Essentials of Buddhism

Ven. Pategama Gnanarama Ph.D.

Principal
Buddhist and Pali College of Singapore

2000

First published in Singapore in 2000

Published by author

ISBN   981-04-2890-1

Printed for free distribution by
The Corporate Body of the Buddha Educational Foundation
11F., 55 Hang Chow South Road Sec 1, Taipei, Taiwan, R.O.C.
Tel: 886-2-23951198 , Fax: 886-2-23913415
Email: overseas@budaedu.org.
Website:http://www.budaedu.org
This book is strictly for free distribution, it is not for sale.

CONTENTS

Introduction and Acknowledgements

Introduction and Acknowledgements

I am thankful to Prof. Oliver Abenayaka who encouraged me to prepare this text in the form of lessons for the students of Than Hsiang Buddhist Temple in Penang, Malaysia. It is based on the Theravada Buddhism syllabus of the Postgraduate Diploma Examination in Buddhist Studies course of the Buddhist and Pali University of Sri Lanka.

Since the work is meant for students, every chapter appears as a unit by itself and is confined to a few pages. The chapters and pages of reference books are given for further reading.

I am also grateful to

- Prof. Gunapala Dharmasiri and Prof. Kapila Abhayawansa for their remarks by way of introducing the book.
- Miss Sumedha Tan for typesetting and formatting the entire work.
- Miss Vajira Quek for going through the proofs and suggesting many alterations in the presentation.
- Ven. Bhikkhuni Sunanda, Prof. Chandima Wijebandara and Dr. (Miss) Gnana Ng Yuen Yen for helping me in numerous ways.
- Last but not least, Ven. W. Ratanasiri Thera and Tisarana Buddhist Association for the unreserved encouragement given to all my Dhamma activities.

P. Gnanarama Thera

Ti-Sarana Buddhist Association
90 Duku Road
Singapore 425294
20/ 7/ 2000

The Fully-Enlightened One

"See the sanity of the man! No gods, no angels, no demons, no body. Nothing of the kind. Stern, sane, every brain-cell perfect and complete even at the moment of death. No delusion."

-*Complete Works of Swamy Vivekananda* III, p. 528

1. *The Buddha in the Pali Canon*

The Buddha, the Fully Enlightened One, was born about two thousand five hundred years ago in the kingdom of Kapilavatthu at the Himalayan Foothills, as the son of the Sakyan king Suddhodana and the queen Mahamaya. His clan name was Gotama (Skt. Gautama) and the name given to him at the naming ceremony attended by many a wise man on the invitation of the king was Siddhattha, (Skt. Siddhārtha) "one who fulfilled the aspiration". A week later his mother died, but a devoted foster-mother was found in his aunt, Mahapajapati Gotami, who also was the king's wife. It was she who brought him up as her own son. It is recorded in the canonical texts that he was brought up in luxury.

As the custom of the day the king made the astrologers and soothsayers assemble to foretell the future of the child. Out of the seven assembled for the occasion six wise men predicted that he would become either a universal monarch or a Buddha, but the youngest of them declared that he would become a Buddha to save mankind from the sufferings of cycle of births and deaths. Then there came a holy sage named Asita to see the baby. Asita with his penetrating wisdom saw the future of the prince Siddhattha and declared:

> "Your son, O king; is one of those rare men born only at rare intervals. A great choice lies before him. He may become a supreme world-ruler, with kings under him, or he may become perfect in wisdom and become a Buddha, an Enlightened One. Truly, O king; I think your son will become a Buddha. But now I am old. I shall not live to

see the glory of your son's achievements nor shall I hear his words of wisdom."

The king was very much moved by the words of Asita. To him there was glory in the thought of his son as ruler of all India and beyond whereas the life of a hermit was mean, cheap and poor in comparison. The king became thoughtful and took every attempt to make the prince's life in the palace a happy and contented one. He was given the best education and was trained to be a king.

One day, King Suddhodana took the prince out to watch the spring ploughing ceremony. At the ceremony the king and some of the nobles took part and drove the oxen when the first furrows were ploughed. Siddhattha was having his own attendants and they sat with him at the side of the field under a rose-apple tree. As he watched he saw his father drive off the royal plough, then the nobles and the farmers following them. When the time came for feasting, his attendants went off to help prepare the feast. Siddhattha was happy to be alone under the shade of a rose-apple tree. There he sat alone, thinking over the day's incidents. He kept on pondering over the oxen that had to drag at the heavy wooden yokes, how the attendants goaded them mercilessly and how the labour made everyone sweat in the heat of the sun. So deeply did he ponder that he began to meditate, his thoughts became concentrated until he forgot his surroundings. When the attendants came back to find him, they saw him seated cross-legged under the tree. So deep were his thoughts that he did not hear them even when they called him, until he came out of his meditation. Years afterwards, Siddhattha was to use the knowledge of concentration that he gained under the rose-apple tree in his strivings to find a solution to life's predicament.

The king was very attentive and made plans to keep his son from the sorrowful side of life. He had three palaces built for three seasons. No servant who was elderly or who had any illness was kept in any of these palaces, and no one was allowed to talk of any sad subject; of death or the loss of dear ones or any kind of unhappiness. According to the traditional custom among the Sakyans, at the age of sixteen, he was married to the Koliyan princess, Yasodhara, after exhibiting his feat of arms in open contest.

Renunciation, Self-Mortification and Enlightenment

Everything went well until he saw the four omens: a sick man, an old man, a corpse and a recluse. The first three omens signify the nature of life symbolically and the fourth was considered as the ideal life to go in search of truth, the remedy for unsatisfactoriness of life. At the age of twenty-nine, after the birth of his son Rahula, he renounced the world to become a recluse. As recorded in the *Ariyapariyesana-sutta* of the *Majjhima-nikaya,* practising meditation under the teacher Alara Kalama he achieved up to the third meditative absorption of Formless sphere and under Uddaka Ramaputta, the fourth meditative absorption of Formless sphere[1]. But realising that it was not what he was searching for, he resorted to extreme forms of self-mortification with the purpose of realising truth. His austere ascetic practices are described in detail in the *Mahāsihanāda-sutta* of the *Majjhima-nikaya*[2]. Later on, after prolonged meditation, he realised the Truth at the age of thirty-five under the

---

[1]   *M.I,* p.160ff.

[2]   *M.I,* p. 68ff.

shade of the *Bodhi* Tree at Buddha Gaya, Gaya. After the enlightenment he was called the Buddha, the Enlightened One or more correctly, *Sammāsambuddha,* the Fully Enlightened One.

The Buddha's Mission

The next forty-five years of His life until His passing away He devoted for the sole purpose of enlightening others. Until the last moment of His mortal existence He followed an active daily routine and spent every second of His life purposefully while enlightening others in the matters related to this life and the next. At the age of eighty, as revealed in the *Mahāparinibbāna-sutta,* He was weak and feeble in body but He was efficient and strong in mind; His self-confidence and determination were fresh as ever[3]. As the *sutta* portrays Him in many an instance, the Buddha in His eighties was failing in physical health due to advanced age and the active life He spent touring many parts of North India while subsisting on whatever food He received at peoples' doorsteps. But He was sound and stable in carrying out the mission He undertook at the age of thirty-five. The *sutta* records a number of instances of His incomparable compassion which He bestowed generously on all as a Teacher par excellence by disseminating freely what He had realised at the foot of the *Bodhi* Tree.

He did not claim any connection with either Brahma or any other gods in the Vedic pantheon. It was when the quest for truth finally resulted in Full Enlightenment He was known as 'Buddha', the epithet by which He was popularly known. Dona, a brahmin, seeing the wheel

[3]   *D. II*, p. 72 ff.

symbol in His footprint, wanted to know who He was and inquired whether He was a god or a *gandhabba* or a demon or a man. Then the Buddha replied that He had destroyed all defilements by which all these different kinds of beings were born and asked the brahmin to take Him to be a Buddha. He compared Himself to a lotus born of mud but unsullied by muddy water; a human born in the world but not of the world. He never claimed that He was a Saviour or a Messiah or a Prophet or a Divine Messenger. But He in referring to His mission humbly asserted that He was only a 'Path Revealer' (*maggakkhāyin*), one who points out the way.

As the last moment of His mortal existence drew nearer the Buddha encouraged the monks to get their doubts cleared, if they had any:

> "If you have any doubt as to the Buddha or the *Dhamma* or the Path or the Method, inquire freely. Do not be depressed afterwards with the thought – our Teacher was with us, but we could not bring ourselves to inquire directly from Him."

For the second and the third time the Buddha insisted that they get their doubts cleared. But nobody spoke up. For the fourth time the Buddha proposed a way of getting their doubts cleared:

> "It may be that you put no question out of reverence for the Teacher. Let your questions be communicated to a friend; so that he may ask me."

But nobody had any question to ask for clarification. For, even the most backward among the gathering was no longer liable to be born in a state of suffering and was assured of attaining sainthood.

Born as prince at the Himalayan Foothills, after a very strenuous search for six years, He attained Enlightenment, the self-illumination without any external help whatsoever. Until the last breath of His life He dedicated Himself to the noble task of enlightening others. Sir Edwin Arnold writing the introduction to his classic *'Light of Asia'* observed three facets of the life of the Buddha blended into one and stated that "He combined the royal qualities of a prince with that of an intellect of a sage and the devotion of a martyr." Certainly, the magnanimous character of the Buddha founded on royal birth, the perfect wisdom that He achieved as the great sage and the dedicated service to enlighten others, made Him supreme.

Salient Features of the Theravada Concept of the Buddha

1. The Buddha was a human being born to human parents in a specific period of history.
2. He was not a Saviour of any kind and not even a Divine Messenger.
3. He attained Enlightenment traversing the path he excavated by Himself.
4. He was an embodiment of compassion *(karunā)* and wisdom *(paññā)*.
5. He was omniscient and He possessed eight kinds of higher knowledges:
   a) Insight *(vidassanā ñāna)*
   b) Knowledge of creating mental images *(manomaya iddhi ñāna)*
   c) Psycho-kinesis *(iddhividha ñāna)*
   d) Clairaudience *(dibbasota)*
   e) Telepathy *(paracittavijānana ñāna)*

f) Antenatal retrocognition (*pubbenivāsānussati ñāna*)

g) Clairvoyance (*dibbacakkhu*)

h) Knowledge of the destruction of defilements (*āsavakkhaya ñāna*)

6. He is endowed with virtuous conduct, which is understood as fifteenfold:

a) Restraint by virtue (*sīla*)

b) Guarding the doors of the sense faculties (*indriyasamvara*)

c) Knowledge of the right amount in eating (*bhojane mattaññutā*)

d) Devotion to wakefulness (*jāgariyānuyoga*)

e) Faith (*saddhā*)

f) Conscience (*hiri*)

g) Moral shame (*ottappa*)

h) Learning (*bāhusacca*)

i) Energy (*parakkama*)

j) Mindfulness (*sati*)

k) Understanding (*mati*)

l) First meditative absorption (*paṭhamajjhāna*)

m) Second meditative absorption (*dutiyajjhāna*)

n) Third meditative absorption (*tatiyajjhāna*)

o) Fourth meditative absorption (*catutthajjhāna*)

7. He preached the oneness of humankind.

8. As a social reformer He elevated the position of women.

9. He preached against caste system and opened the doors of His dispensation to all.

10. He became Buddha by perfecting all the ten Perfections in his previous births.

📖📖📖

Impermanence of All Phenomena

Master Assaji to Saccaka:

> "This is how the Blessed One disciplines his disciples, Aggivessana, and this is how the Blessed One's instruction is usually presented to his disciples:
>
> 'Bhikkhus, material form is impermanent, feeling is impermanent, perception is impermanent, formations are impermanent, consciousness is impermanent.'"

-Cūlasaccaka-sutta, M. I, p.228
MLDB. p. 322

2. *Impermanence as a Basic Fact of Existence*

I mpermanence (*anicca*), Unsatisfactoriness (*dukkha*) and Egolessness (*anatta*) are basic facts of existence. Collectively these three are named in Buddhism as 'Three Signata' (*ti-lakkhaṇa*) or 'Three Characteristics of Existence'. At the outset it is plausible to see how these three doctrines have been explained in relation to one another in the *Anattalakkhaṇa-sutta*, the second discourse delivered by the Buddha after His Enlightenment[1]. The discourse in question was addressed to the first five converts. The discourse clearly shows the arguments adduced by the Buddha to establish these three fundamental characteristics of existence.

Arguments Adduced in the *Anattalakkhaṇa-sutta*

Addressing the five monks the Buddha said:

> "Body, monks, is not self. Now, were this body self, monks, this body would not tend to sickness, and one might get the chance of saying in regard to the body, 'Let body become thus for me'. But inasmuch, monks, as body is not self, therefore body tends to sickness, and one does not get the chance of saying in regard to the body, 'Let body become thus for me, let body not become thus for me'. Feeling is not

---

[1]   *S. III*, p. 66; *Vin. I*. pp. 13-14. As the discourse was addressed to a group of five ascetics, it is called '*Pañca-sutta*' in the *Samyuttanikaya*.

self..........and one does not get the chance of saying in regard to feeling, 'Let feeling become thus for me, let feeling not become thus for me'. Perception is not self...; mental formations are not self...; consciousness is not self.... Inasmuch, monks, as consciousness is not self, therefore consciousness tends to sickness, and one does not get the chance to say in regard to consciousness, 'Let consciousness become thus for me, let consciousness not become thus for me'. What do you think about this monks? Is body permanent or impermanent?"

Then the dialogue follows:

"Impermanent, Lord."
"But is that which is impermanent sorrowful (*dukkha*) or happy (*sukha*)?"
"Sorrowful, Lord."
"But is it fit to consider that which is impermanent, sorrowful, of a nature to change, as 'This is mine, this am I, this is my self'?"
"It is not, Lord."
"Is feeling.......perception.......mental formations........ consciousness permanent or impermanent?"
"Impermanent, Lord."
"But is that which is impermanent sorrowful or happy?"
"Sorrowful, Lord."
"But is it fit to consider that which is impermanent, sorrowful, of a nature to change, as 'This is mine, this am I, this is my self?"
"It is not so, Lord."
"Wherefore, monks, whatever is body, past, future, present, internal or external, gross or subtle, low or excellent, whether it is far or near........whatever is feeling.........whatever is perception........whatever is

mental formation......-all should, by means of right wisdom, be seen, as it really is, thus: This is not mine, this am I not, this is not my self."

"Seeing in this way, monks, the instructed disciple of the *Ariyans* disregards body, feeling, perception, mental formations, and consciousness; disregarding, he is dispassionate; through dispassion he is freed; in freedom he acquires the knowledge that 'I am freed' and he knows that 'destroyed is birth, there is no more being as such and such'."

Empirical Observation of Facts

The importance of the foregoing discourse, for the study of Buddhist doctrine of the basic characteristics of existence, is highly valued for several reasons. The characteristics of impermanence, unsatisfactoriness and non-substantiality have been established in the discourse not as a result of any kind of metaphysical inquiry or as an outcome of any mystical intuition. It is a judgement arrived at by observation, investigation and analysis of empirical data. The method followed in achieving the basic facts of existence is inductive as opposed to deductive method of reasoning. On the other hand the three characteristics are inter-related and inter-woven with one another. So much so one establishes the reality of the other two. The fact of Impermanence proves the facts of Unsatisfactoriness and Non-Substantiality and the fact of Unsatisfactoriness on the other hand establishes the validity of Impermanence and the theory of Non-Substantiality. The theory of Non-Substantiality or Egolessness verifies the reality of Impermanence and Unsatisfactoriness. Hence the three basic concepts of Buddhist doctrine, Impermanence, Unsatisfactoriness and

Non-Substantiality have been proved on the mutual support of each individual characteristic. As stated in a different context that which is transient is unsatisfactory (*yad aniccaṁ taṁ dukkhaṁ* and that which is unsatisfactory is no-self (*yaṁ dukkhaṁ tadanattā*). The theory as a whole exhausts the world-view of Buddhism. The discourse being a dialogue between the Buddha and the group of five monks converted at the outset of the Buddha's mission elucidates the fundamental facts of empiric individuality as plainly as possible, avoiding any kind of metaphysical reasoning.

Etymological and Doctrinal Meaning of the Term *'anicca'*

The term *'anicca'* is an adjective usually used in the sense of a noun. *'Aniccaṁ'* is the neuter noun used in the language. Both the words are prefixed with negative 'a'. Therefore the word means 'impermanent' or 'impermanence', used as the antonym of *'nicca'*(*na niccan'ti aniccaṁ*). But in the *Abhidhamma* commentaries the derivation of the word has been traced to root 'i' to go. With the prefix 'an' giving the meanings 'cannot be gone to', 'unapproachable as a permanent everlasting state'. The term has the applied meanings of 'unstability', 'impermanence', and 'inconstancy'. The *Visuddhimagga* defines it as 'that which is not permanent (*nicca*) is impermanent (*anicca*)' (*na niccaṁ aniccaṁ*).[2] The commentary on the *Dhammasangini* defines it as 'that which having come into being ceases to be' (*hutvā abhāvaṭṭhena*).[3] The transient character of all things mental or material is an emphatic assertion found

---

[2]   *Vis.* p. 525
[3]   *DhsA.* iv, 85

throughout the Buddhist doctrine. The correct understanding of it, is a primary condition for right knowledge.

Impermanence: the Nature of all Component Things

When we confine ourselves to the first of the three characteristics, we see that Impermanence or transient nature of all phenomena finds expression in the canon in numerous contexts. For instance we come across in the *Mahāparinibbāna-sutta*:

> "Impermanent are all component things,
> They arise and cease, that is their nature,
> They come into being and pass away,
> Release from them is bliss supreme".[4]

The discernment of the transient nature of all compounded things as they really are (*yathābhūta*), is taught as the path to purity. It is said in the *Dhammapada*:

> "Transient are all component things; when this with wisdom, one discerns, then one is disgusted with unsatisfactoriness; this is the path to purity".[5]

It is to be noted that the Pali word used for component things is *'sankhāra'*, which has different meanings. It is used in the present context to mean what is compounded, conditioned and causally arisen. According to Buddhist analysis every phenomenon of our

---

[4] *D. II,* p. 157
[5] *Dhp.*277

experience is causally conditioned. *Nibbāna* alone is beyond causal nexus.[6]

In the canon very striking similes have been drawn to bring out the ephemeral nature of the five aggregates of empiric individuality: corporeality (*rupa*), sensation (*vedanā*), perception (*saññā*), mental formations (*sankhāra*) and consciousness (*viññāna*). The Buddha compares corporeality to a lump of foam, feeling to a bubble, perception to a mirage, mental formation to a plantain trunk (which is pithless) and consciousness to an illusion and says:

> "What essence, monks, could there be in a lump of foam, in a bubble, in a mirage, in a plantain trunk, and in an illusion?"

The Buddha continues:

> "Whatever corporeality there be - whether past, present, or future; internal or external; gross or subtle; low or lofty; far or near - that corporeality, the monk sees, meditates upon, examines with systematic attention. He thus seeing, meditating upon, and examining with systematic attention, would find it empty, he would find it unsubstantial and without essence. What essence, monks, could there be in corporeality?"

In the same vein, He refers to the remaining four aggregates and asks:

---

[6] See Nyanatiloka Ven. - *Buddhist Dictionary* for further annotations

"What essence, monks, could there be in feeling, in perception, in mental formations, and in consciousness?"[7]

Therefore in Buddhism the sum total of the teaching of Impermanence is that all component things that have conditioned existence are a process and not a group of abiding entities, but the change occurs in such a rapid succession, one does not perceive their arising (*udaya*) and breaking up (*vaya*). Therefore tends to regard mind and body as static entities. It has been shown that people are accustomed to thinking their own mind and body and the external world as wholes or discrete entities. So long as one fails to see things as processes in motion, one will not understand transient nature of all phenomena. When one sees things as they really are, one realises that life is a mere flux conditioned by internal and external causes. As everything is fleeting, nowhere can one find happiness but only unsatisfactoriness. It is to be noted that always the three characteristics are mutually inclusive and the proof of one proves the other two. Knowledge of Insight (*vidassanā-ñāna*) is attained by realising the Three Signata.

Is Consciousness Soul?

Consciousness has been taken to mean soul or ego by the Upanishadic philosophers. This view was upheld by some of the disciples during the time of the Buddha. As recorded in the *Mahatanhasankhaya-sutta* of the *Majjhima-nikaya*, a monk called Sati misunderstood the teaching of the Buddha and held the view that consciousness is a permanent entity that passes from one

---

[7]   *S.* III, p. 140

existence to another. His concept of consciousness (*viññāṇa*) is similar to *'nirāsraya vijñāna'* discussed in the Upanishads. In this instance the Buddha stated categorically that there is no arising of consciousness without relative conditions (*aññatra paccayā natthi viññāṇassa sambhavo*).[8] In another context too, the consideration of consciousness as a permanent entity has been criticised by the Buddha. For He states:

> "It were better O monks; if the ignorant and untaught manyfolk regards the body, which is composed of the four elements as ego, rather than the mind. And why do I say so? Because it is evident, O monks, that this body which is composed of four elements lasts one year, lasts two years, lasts three years, four, five, ten, twenty, thirty years, lasts for forty years, lasts fifty years, hundred years and even longer. But that which is called the mind, intellect, consciousness keeps up an incessant round by day and by night of perishing as one thing, and springing up as another".[9]

The Buddha's last words to the monks was also a reminder of the truth of impermanence:

> "Indeed, O monks, I declare to you, decay is inherent in all component things. Strive for perfection through heedfulness".[10]

ꔰ ꔰ ꔰ

---

8   *M.I*, p. 256
9   *S.II*, p. 96
10   *D.II*, p. 144

Pervasive Unsatisfactoriness

"While 'suffering' is the conventional translation for the Buddha's word *dukkha*, it does not really do the word justice. A more specific translation would be something on the order of 'pervasive unsatisfactoriness'. The Buddha is speaking on a number of levels here. Life, he says, is filled with a sense of pervasive unsatisfactoriness, stemming from at least three sources."

-Mark Epstein
Thoughts without a Thinker, p. 46

3. The Concept of Dukkha in Early Buddhist Teaching

'*Dukkha*' is the second fundamental characteristic of existence and the First Noble Truth of the list of Four Noble Truths. The term '*dukkha*' has been used in Buddhist teaching to convey the totality of experiences of a normal human being in the world. It has been rendered into English in numerous ways. The common rendering being 'suffering', many more different English words are being used by different Buddhist scholars to convey the meaning of the original Pali term. Among them, the words 'ill', 'pain', 'sorrow', 'insecurity', 'unpleasantness', 'anguish', 'anxiety', 'unhappiness', 'conflict', and 'unsatisfactoriness' are found. Today, the most commonly used words in Buddhist writings for the term '*dukkha*', are 'suffering' and 'unsatisfactoriness'. In this book, wherever necessary we also will use those two words. The antonym of '*dukkha*' is '*sukha*', which is translated often as 'bliss', 'pleasure' or 'happiness'. In Buddhist usage it is not merely sensual pleasure, it is the happy feeling in ordinary sense. But it is also used to convey an ethical import of doctrinal significance. In Pali, many other words are used to bring out the import of suffering. Sorrow *(soka)*, lamentation *(parideva)*, pain *(dukkha)*, grief *(domanassa)*, and despair *(upāyāsa)* are the most popularly used. The concept of suffering necessarily includes the general insecurity of the whole of our experience.

The Etymological Definition and the Exegesis

Buddhaghosa explaining the derivation of the term in the *Visuddhimagga* says:

> "The word *'du'* ('bad') is met within the sense of vile *(kucchita)*; for they call a vile child a *'duputta'* (bad child). The word *'kham'* ('-ness'), however, is met within the sense of empty *(tuccha)*, for they call empty space *'kham'*. And the First Truth is vile because it is the haunt of many dangers, and empty because it is devoid of the lastingness, beauty, pleasure and self, conceived by rash people. So it is called *'dukkham'* ('badness'= suffering, pain), because of vileness and emptiness."[1]

It has been classified further into three aspects for better understanding:

I.   Intrinsic suffering *(dukkha-dukkha)*
II.   Suffering in change *(viparināma-dukkha)*
III. Suffering due to formation *(sankhāra-dukkha)*

Bodily and mental painful feeling are called intrinsic suffering because of their individual essence, their name and painfulness. Bodily and mental pleasant feeling are called suffering in change because they are a cause for the arising of pain when they change. Feeling of equanimity and the remaining formations of the three planes are called suffering due to formation because, they are oppressed by rise and fall. Such bodily and mental affliction as earache, toothache, fever born of lust, fever born of hate, etc., is called concealed suffering

---

[1]   *Vis.* p. 494 and p. 499; *M. I* p. 303

because it can only be known by questioning and because the infliction is not openly evident. It is also called suffering not evident. The affliction produced by the thirty-two tortures etc., is called exposed suffering because it can be known without questioning and because the infliction is openly evident; it is also called evident suffering. Except for intrinsic suffering, all given in the exposition of the truth of suffering beginning with birth are also called indirect suffering because they are the basis for one kind of suffering or another.[2] Intrinsic suffering is called direct suffering.[3]

Physiological, Psychological and Doctrinal Applications of the Term

Suffering or unsatisfactoriness *(dukkha)* as described in the scriptures has a wider connotation. It has been used to denote a narrow physical meaning as well as a psychological meaning side by side with a usage of doctrinal import. All these three applications of the term is quite clearly seen in the analysis of suffering found in the first discourse of the Buddha addressed to the first five converts at Isipatana, Benares. Explaining the First Noble Truth, which is named as the Noble Truth of Suffering, the Buddha continued:

> "And this, monks, is the Noble Truth of Suffering: birth is suffering, old age is suffering, disease is suffering and dying is suffering, association with what is not dear is suffering, separation from what is dear is suffering, not getting what one wants is suffering - in short the five aggregates of

---

[2] *Vibhanga* p. 99; See also *The Path* XVI, 16, pp. 32-43
[3] *Vis.* p. 499

grasping   *(pañca-upādanakkhandha)*   are
suffering." [4]

This is a very precise statement full of meaning covering all spheres of human life, which delineates the influence of suffering in many aspects. Firstly, birth, old age, disease and death have been mentioned to illustrate the physiological aspect of the issue. Secondly, the psychological aspect has been brought to light by the facts of association of what is not dear, separation from what is dear and not getting what one wants and thirdly, the doctrinal aspect is stated by the fact of the five aggregates of grasping. What Buddhaghosa explained in the *Visuddhimagga* as intrinsic suffering *(dukkha-dukkha)*, suffering in change *(viparināma-dukkha),* and suffering due to formation *(sankhāra-dukkha)* are found implicit in this description. Therefore in a broader sense all aspects of suffering brought to light in the discourse in question are mutually inclusive. Therefore it is expressed as a unitary concept in Buddhism exhausting every facet of human existence. Concealed suffering, exposed suffering or evident suffering, direct suffering and indirect suffering described by Buddhaghosa are exegetical elaborations of the original concept of the teaching on doctrinal grounds.

The first two aspects called the physiological and the psychological aspects of suffering are quite clear. The doctrinal aspect of suffering is stated in brief in the discourse referring to five aggregates of grasping, namely:

    i.   grasping of materiality *(rūpa upādāna)*
    ii. grasping of feeling *(vedanā upādāna)*
    iii. grasping of perception *(saññā upādāna)*

---

[4]   *Vin.* I, p. 10

    iv. grasping of mental formation *(sankhāra upādāna)*

    v. grasping of consciousness *(viññāna upādāna)*

In other words, holding on to five constituent factors of empiric individuality, whether they are internal or external cause suffering. By the five terms, the aspects of materiality or corporeality, sensation, perception, conation and cognition are to be understood. In fact, the classification of five aggregates covers the entire phenomenal existence. How they cause proliferation *(papañca)* ultimately leading to suffering is described graphically in the Buddhist theory of perception found in early Buddhism as well as in the later *Abhidhamma* philosophy in a much more elaborate form. It is to be noted, however, that which leads to suffering are not the five aggregates but the mental process of grasping *(upa+ā+√dā)* thereof. Suffering that one has to experience in one's wanderings in the cycle of existence has to be understood in this doctrinal basis and not on the constituent factors of individuality.

Now let us examine how these sufferings are described with additional items in the *Saccavibhanga-sutta* of the *Majjhima-nikaya*. The discourse gives the following description describing each item that contributes to suffering:

1. Birth *(jāti)*
    The birth of beings into the various orders of beings, their coming to birth, precipitation in a womb, generation, the manifestation of the aggregates, obtaining the bases for contact.

2. Aging *(jāra)*
   The aging of beings in the various orders of beings, their old age, brokenness of teeth, greyness of hair, wrinkling of skin, decline of life, weakness of faculties.

3. Death *(maraṇa)*
   The passing of beings out of the various orders of beings, their passing away, dissolution, disappearance, dying, completion of time, dissolution of aggregates, laying down of the body.

4. Sorrow *(soka)*
   The sorrow, sorrowing, sorrowfulness, inner sorrow, and inner sorrowfuless of one who has encountered some misfortune or is affected by some painful state.

5. Lamentation *(parideva)*
   The wail and lament, wailing and lamenting, bewailing and lamentation of one who has encountered some misfortune or is affected by some painful state.

6. Pain *(dukkha)*
   Bodily pain, bodily discomfort, painful, uncomfortable feeling born of bodily contact.

7. Grief *(domanassa)*
   Mental pain, mental discomfort, painful, uncomfortable feeling born of mental contact.

8. Despair *(upāyāsa)*
   The trouble and despair, the tribulation and desperation of one who has encountered some misfortune or is affected by some painful state.

9. Not to obtain what one wants is suffering *(yam pi icchaṁ na labhati)*
   The fact that the above situations cannot be averted by mere wishing.

10. Five   aggregates   of   grasping   *(pañca*
    upādānakkhandha)
    Material form, feeling, perception, thought formation
    and consciousness affected by clinging, in short, are
    suffering. [5]

Three Kinds of Feeling

In a broader sense, Buddhism identifies three kinds of
feeling: Happy *(sukha)*, Sorrowful *(dukkha)* and
Equanimous *(upekkhā)*. Happy feeling that one
experiences in one's life may turn to be unhappy
afterwards. Sorrowful feeling may turn to be happy due
to some reason or other. A person who is hungry is
happy when he is fed. But he is not able to retain that
happiness forever. Again he will be hungry and he is to
be fed. The same is the procedure with regard to change
of postures. A person who keeps standing for along time
finds it happy for him to sit down comfortably. But it is
not possible for him to keep on sitting all the time. Soon
he finds that it is comfortable for him to change the
posture. This means that these feelings are transitory and
superficial. There is the universal truth of suffering
underlying all these feelings. So it is clear that suffering
(dukkha) has been used in a narrow, superficial sense as
well as in a broad philosophical sense; which is nothing
but impermanence *(yaṁ aniccaṁ taṁ dukkhaṁ).*

Each of the aggregates of individuality is in a constant
flux and there is no one's 'own-ness' in any of them.
Therefore the Buddhist dictum 'that which is
impermanent is suffering' is to be considered as a
universal truth.

---

[5]   *M.* III, p. 249

Suffering one has to encounter throughout one's life is self-evident for the most part, and needs no elaboration. In other words, one is overwhelmed by unsatisfactory and conflicting situations that one experiences in one's day to day life and needs no comment. Because the internal and external conflicts that one has to face throughout one's life are signified by the concept of suffering in Buddhism, some are of the opinion that 'conflict' is the best English word that carries full import of the Pali word.

To a greater extent, the cultivation of right attitude to life will ease some of the suffering that one has to encounter, because it is obvious that wrong attitude to life contributes much of the suffering. Feeling of something lacking looms large in our lives. Until it is filled, it keeps on causing pain. But when it is filled, a new void is created and produces suffering until it is satisfied. Pleasure we anticipated vanishes, no sooner than it is produced, and new expectations then arise contributing to mental pain again. New acquisitions, which produce happiness and pleasure for a certain period of time, give rise to disappointment, despair and frustration.

Different Kinds of Happiness

Buddhism speaks of different kinds of happiness. Monks' happiness *(pabbajjā- sukha)* is contrasted with laymen's happiness *(gihi-sukha)*. In the same way happiness of sensual enjoyment *(kāma-sukha)* is contrasted with happiness of renunciation *(nekkhamma-sukha)*. Similarly, happiness of acquisition *(upadhi-sukha)*, happiness of having influxes *(sāsava-sukha)*, physical happiness *(kāyika-sukha)* are contrasted with happiness of non-acquisition *(nirupadhi-sukha)*, happiness of

2 222 2222222222222222

freedom from influxes (*anāsava-sukha*) and mental happiness (*cetasikha-sukha*).

📖📖📖

Suffering!

Man is yoked to the kammic cart,
Suffering rolls on behind his feet,
Carrot is hanging in front of his nose,
But with hopes he forges ahead.
Drags the cart on rugged path,
Until at last meet with death!

P. Gnanarama

Non-Substantiality of Phenomena

Then, when it was morning, the Blessed one dressed, and taking his bowl and outer robe, went into Savatthi for alms. The venerable Rahula also dressed, and taking his bowl and outer robe, followed close behind the Blessed One.

Then the Blessed one looked back and addressed the venerable Rahula thus:

> "Rahula, any kind of material form whatever, whether past, future or present, internal or external, gross or subtle, inferior or superior, far or near, all material form should be seen as it actually is with proper wisdom thus: 'This is not mine, this am I not, this is not my self.'"

-Mahārāhulovāda-sutta, M. I, 421-2

MLDB, p. 527

4. *The Theory of Egolessness (anatta) in Early Buddhism*

The theory of egolessness *(anatta)* is the third of the Three Characteristics of Existence taught in early Buddhism. In order to denote the antonym of Ego *(atta)*, the English words, 'Soul', 'Self', 'Substantiality', and 'Entity' are also used. Therefore the Buddhist theory of Egolessness is often discussed as the theory of 'No-Soul', or 'No-Self', or 'Non-Substantiality', or 'No-Entity'. Here we also invariably use these words to denote the Buddhist teaching on Egolessness *(anatta)* as found in the early Buddhist canonical scriptures.

It should be noted at the beginning what is denoted by the word *'atta'* and what it does not connote, in the teaching of the Buddha. In Pali, the word has been used in no less than five meanings:

1. As 'oneself' in the conventional sense. (e.g., *attā hi attano nātho)*
2. As one's own person including both physical and mental aspects of a person. (e.g., *attabhāvapaṭilābha)*
3. 'Self' as a subtle metaphysical entity. (e.g., *atthi me attā)*
4. Enclitic *'-atta'*, in the sense of '-ness'. (e.g., *socitattaṁ)*
5. As a result of phonetical convergence on the Sanskrit word *'āpta',* meaning 'obtained'.(e.g., *attaṁ nirattaṁ na hi tassa hoti)*

The fact that the word *'atta'* has been used in the canon in the sense of 'Ego' or 'Self', only when referred to the theory of soul held by other religionists of the day is clear. In many other instances it carries only the conventional sense of 'oneself'. Those who have not properly understood the different implications of the word tend to assert otherwise. The Buddhist theory of egolessness teaches that neither within the body nor within the mental phenomena and external phenomena can be found an entity, self-existing, abiding, immutable substance called 'Self'. No manikin, 'a man in man', is found as maintained by *Katha Upanisad* which has referred to a man or principle *(purusa)* of the size of thumb residing always in the heart of man. The theory of egolessness is a fundamental Buddhist doctrine having particular significance in Buddhism. The impersonality of all existence has been established on the basis of continual self-consuming process of arising and passing of bodily and mental phenomena. It has been shown that within or without this process there is no entity which can be taken as self in terms of 'this is mine' *(etaṁ mama)*, 'this am I' *(eso hamasmi)* and 'this is my self' *(eso me attā)*.

Monism in Indian Philosophy

The theory of soul is deep-rooted in Indian thought and found even in the Vedas. As the *Rig Veda*, the earliest religious document in India, reveals the belief of a monistic principle has given rise to the concept of soul (presented as *brahman* and *ātman*) in later times. The Hymn of Creation [1] found in the *Rig Veda* is considered important in this regard. It speaks of 'That One' *(tad ekaṁ)* which was at the beginning. Its spontaneous unfolding into everything is described in the hymn. It

[1]   *RV. X, 129*

was impersonal and free from mythological elements. It was the unitary world ground, the First Cause as they thought.

During the time of *Upanisads*, many speculative theories were formulated to explain the nature of soul. As described in the *Chandogya Upanisad*, soul is free from death, free from sorrow, and having real thoughts. Then, the soul was recognised as the physical personality, which is seen reflected in a pan of water. But this physical personality, it is argued on empirical grounds, is subject to death; therefore it cannot be soul. Then the soul is identified with self in the dream-state. Again, it is identified with the state of deep sleep. In different stages of the development of the concept different names were given for its identification. Individual soul or microcosmic soul (*pratyagātman* or *pudgalātman*) was differentiated from macrocosmic soul (*jagadātman*). The individual souls were considered as the manifestations of the macrocosmic soul. The whole universe is a manifestation of the macrocosm. It is said, in the beginning *Sat* (Being) was alone, without a second. It thought: "May I be many". Now it diversified into the three elements: fire (*tejas*), water (*āp*), earth (*prthivi*) and then into others until organic bodies, including those of human beings, have come into being. The various aspects of the monistic principle have been elaborately discussed in different *Upanisad texts* in numerous ways.

The theory is summarised in the *Bhagavad-Gitā* to illustrate the migration of self from one body to another and compared it to a person wearing a new garment, casting away the worn out one. It is unborn and it does not die. It is primeval and eternal, it is not destroyed even when the body is destroyed. It can never be cut to pieces by any weapon, nor burned by fire, nor moistened by water, nor withered by the wind.[2]

The Buddhist Criticism of the Theory of Ego

The theory of ego has been criticised in Buddhism together with another famous view at the time. Those who ascribed eternity and immutability to ego were called eternalists *(sassatavādin)* and those who rejected the theory on empirical grounds were called nihilists or materialists *(ucchedavādin)*. According to eternalism body is one and the soul is another *(aññam jivaṁ aññaṁ saīiraṁ)*. As the soul is imprisoned in the body pending release for the union with the universal soul, one has to practise penance for its release. In the *Brahmajāla-sutta* of the *Digha-nikaya* no less than fifty-five eternalist theories have been mentioned. The nihilists or the materialists on the other hand held the view that the body and the soul are one *(taṁ jivaṁ taṁ sariraṁ)*, and that the soul is only a psycho-physical unit which does not survive death. With the death of a person his soul also perishes. Therefore they advocated the indulgence in sensual pleasures. Seven kinds of nihilist theories have been mentioned in the *Brahmajāla-sutta*. These two views are diametrically opposed to each other and named as extremes. The arguments of impermanence and suffering adduced in the *Anattalakkhana-sutta* prove that the view is untenable on empirical grounds. The three concepts: impermanence

---

[2]   *Vāsāṁsi jīrṇāni yathā vihāya – navāni grhnāti naro parāni*
       Tathā sarīrān vihāya jīrṇān – anyāni samyāti navāni dehi
       – 2.22
       Nainaṁ chindati sastrāni – nainaṁ dahati pāvako
       Na cainaṁ kledayantyāpo – na sosyati mārutah – 2.23

(anicca), suffering *(dukkha),* and egolessness *(anatta)* are inter-related and inter-mingled, which the discourse in question has attested with adequate proofs.

In the canon, the problem of rebirth is explained on the teaching of Dependent Origination; which itself is sufficient to show in which way one existence is connected with former and future existences. It is explained in the teaching that the real connecting link between one existence and another is not the so called 'ego' or any kind of soul substance, but *kamma.* The Buddha says:

> "This, O monks, is not your body, nor that of others. You have rather to see in it, monks, old deeds *(kamma),* the result of actions; volitions and feelings in former existences."[3]

There is scriptural evidence to show that the Buddha has not maintained any kind of soul substance, as professed by the Brahmanas and other ascetics, recluses and founders of religious sects of His day.

Five Aggregates are Conditioned

When the question of who is that feels was put to Him, the Buddha answered:

> "This question is not proper. Because I do not teach that there is one who feels. If, however, the question is put thus:- Conditioned through what, does feeling arise? Then the answer will be:- Through sense-impression is feeling

---
[3] *S. XII, 37*

conditioned...... through feeling, craving; through craving, clinging;.........." [4]

Doctrine of Egolessness as via Media

The Buddha states:

> "I do not teach that there is one thing called old age and death, and that there is someone to whom they belong. Verily, if one holds the view that life (*jīva*=life principle, soul) is identical with the body (*tam jīvam tam sarīram*), in that case there can be no holy life. And if one holds the view that life is one thing but body another thing (*aññam jīvam aññam sarīram*), also in that case holy life is impossible. Avoiding both of these extremes (i.e. complete identity and complete otherness) the Perfect One has taught the doctrine that lies in the middle, namely: Through rebirth conditioned are old age and death; ......through the process of becoming, rebirth;..... through clinging, the process of becoming;....... etc." [5]

Body and Mind are Devoid of Ego

> "Better it would be to consider the body as the ego rather than the mind. And why? Because this body may last for ten, twenty, thirty, forty, or fifty years, even for hundred years and more. But that

---

[4]   *S. XII,* 12
[5]   *S.XII,* 35

which is called mind, consciousness, thinking (*citta=mana=viññāṇa*), arises continuously during day and night as one thing, and then as something else it vanishes. Here the learned and noble disciple considers thoroughly the Dependent Origination: when this arises then that arises. Through the arising of this, that comes to arise; through the extinction of this, that becomes extinguished, namely: Through ignorance arise the *kamma*-formations; through the *kamma*-formations, consciousness (in next life); through consciousness, corporeality and mind..............etc." [6]

Ignorant Worldlings Seek Ego in the Individual Factors of the Five Aggregates

"All those ascetics and brahmins, who again and again in manifold ways believe in an ego or the ego as the owner of that group. They all do so with regard to the five aggregates of existence, or to one of them......... There the ignorant worldling......... considers, one of the five aggregates as the ego, or the ego as the owner of that aggregate, or that aggregates as included in the ego, or the ego as included in that aggregate." [7]

---

[6]   *S. XII, 61*
[7]   *S. XIII, 47*

The Totality of Five Aggregates is not Ego

"The learned and noble disciple does not consider corporeality, feeling, perception, mental formations, or consciousness as the ego; nor ego as the owner of one of these aggregates, nor these aggregates as included within the ego, nor the ego as included within the aggregates. Of such a learned and noble disciple it is said that he is no longer fettered by any aggregate of existence, internal or external."[8]

The World is Empty of an Ego

To the question why does one call the world empty, answer is given:

"Because the world is empty of an ego *(atta)*, and of something belonging to the ego *(attaniya)*, therefore the world is called empty. But which are the things that are empty of an ego? Empty of an ego are the eye and visible objects, ear and sounds, nose and odours, tongue and tastes, body and bodily impressions, mind and mind objects" [9]

Consciousness is Egoless

"............... consciousness (mind) is egoless. Also the causes and conditions arising from

---

[8]   *S. XXII, 117*
[9]   *S. XXXV, 85*

consciousness are likewise egoless. Then how
could it be possible that consciousness having
arisen through something, which is egoless, could
ever be an ego?" [10]

At first sight the concept of responsibility appears to be
incompatible with the doctrine of soullessness. Since
there is textual evidence refuting the seeming
discrepancy, it is not to be taken seriously. It is stated
that a certain monk entertained the thought that since
body, feeling, perception, mental formations and
consciousness is without self, could deeds not done by a
self, affect. This supposition amounts to saying that if
there is no self, there can be no personal identity and no
personal responsibility. This is dismissed as an
unwarranted corollary of, or as going against the teaching
of the Buddha.[11] In many instances in the canon, the fact
of responsibility is explained on the doctrine of
Dependent Origination. The above quotations show that
the theory of Egolessness is a specific Buddhist teaching.

📖📖📖

Aryan Disciple and Non-substantiality

*"The instructed disciple of the Aryan beholds of material
shape and so on this way: 'This is not mine, this am I not,
this is not my self.' So when the material shape and so on
change and become otherwise there arise not for him grief,
sorrow, suffering, lamentation and despair."*

-S.,III, p.19

---

[10] *S. XXV,* 141
[11] *M. III,* p. 19

Illusion of Self-Sufficiency

"In his teachings on suffering, the Buddha made clear that some kind of humiliation awaits us all. This is the truth that he felt could be apprehended by those with 'little dust in their eyes'. No matter what we do, he taught, we cannot sustain the illusion of our self-sufficiency. We are all subject to decay, old age, and death, to disappointment, loss, and disease. We are all engaged in a futile struggle to maintain ourselves in our own image. The crisis in our lives inevitably reveal how impossible our attempts to control our destinies really are."

-Mark Epstein
Thoughts without a Thinker, p. 44

5. *The First Noble Truth: Suffering (dukkha sacca)*

The Four Noble Truths are given in brief in the first discourse named the "Turning of the Wheel of Law" (*Dhammacakkappavattana-sutta*), delivered at Isipatana, in Benares, by the Buddha after His Enlightenment. It is interesting to note that the *sutta* begins by showing the futility of the two extreme practices prevailing among the truth seekers of the day. The first of the two practices mentioned in the discourse was based on materialism (*uccheda-vāda*) and the other was on eternalism (*sassata-vāda*).

The Two Extremes are to be Avoided by a Truth-Seeker

Addressing the five ascetics with whom He had association when He practised austere asceticism as Bodhisatta, the Buddha says that there are two extremes to be avoided by a recluse who is seeking realisation.

The two extremes are self-indulgence (*kāmasukhallikānuyoga*) and self-mortification (*attakilamathānuyoga*). Attachment to worldly enjoyment in respect of sensual pleasures is low (*hino*), common (*gammo*), belonging to ordinary man (*pothujjaniko*), ignoble (*anariyo*), and connected with misery (*anatthasamhito*). Self-mortification is (full of) suffering (*dukkho*), ignoble (*anariyo*), and connected with misery (*anatthasamhito*). Although five adjectives have been used for the former and three for the latter with reference to the basis of ideology on which they were founded for the purpose of realising truth, the two extreme practices are comparatively useless. (The word *'anatthasamhita'* also means futility).

The Buddha points out the Middle Path *(majjhimā patipadā)* lying between these two extremes, produces insight and knowledge leading to serenity, higher knowledge, full enlightenment and Supreme Bliss, *Nibbāna*. Then the discourse summarises the eight factors of the Middle Path and moves on to reveal the Four Noble Truths: The Suffering or Unsatisfactoriness *(dukkha)*, the Cause of Suffering *(dukkha-samudaya)*, the Cessation of Suffering *(dukkha-nirodha)*, and the Path Leading to the Cessation of Suffering *(dukkha-nirodhagāmini-patipadā)*.

The discourse reveals that the Four Noble Truths are three-circled and twelvefold *(tiparivattam dvādasākāram)*. With regard to each truth, there is the knowledge of the truth *(sacca-ñāṇa)*, the knowledge that it is to be comprehended *(kicca-ñāṇa)*, and the knowledge of comprehension *(kata-ñāṇa)* which arose in the Buddha, thus making the knowledge twelvefold by three circles of each truth.[1]

Why are They Called 'Noble' and 'Truths'?

Acariya Buddhaghosa, the famous commentator, explains the First Noble Truth in no less than fifteen ways.

According to him these are called Noble Truths because the Noble Ones, the Buddhas etc., penetrate them.

[1]   *S. IV,* p. 420 ff;   *Vin.* I, p. 10 ff.

Besides, Noble Truths are the Noble One's truths. Or alternatively, they are called Noble Truths because of the nobleness implied by their discovery. And further, to be noble is to be not unreal; the meaning is, not deceptive, as it is said, "Bhikkhus, these Four Noble Truths are real, not unreal, not otherwise, that is why they are called Noble Truths."[2] Therefore the adjective *'ariya'* is used in this context to mean 'noble' and not to convey any ethnic or racial sense at all.

What is meant by truth? The word truth *(sacca)* has been used in various meanings in the Pali canon. For example, when it is said, "Let him speak truth and not be angry", it is verbal truth. In the same way, the word has been used in the sense of truth of abstinence, views, ultimate truth and noble truth.[3] A truth is a factual statement, which is correspondent with the real state of affairs and coherent with what is existing factually. These truths are factual, real, and can be experienced as veritable truths.

The Dhamma is Compared to Medicine

Very often, the Buddha's preaching of the doctrine, to the suffering world, is compared to the administration of medicine to the sick by a physician. Therefore the expounding of the Four Noble Truths in the first sermon can be understood on the analogy of a pathological analysis of affliction and cure. Therein the present predicament of man is analysed in the First Noble Truth with its physical, psychological and doctrinal aspects and shows how those afflictions are woven into the fabric of our existence. The discourse gives in brief the physical

[2] *Vis. XVI*, pp. 14-22
[3] *Vis. XVI*, p. 26

aspect of affliction stating the facts of birth, old age, disease and death. Association with the unpleasant, separation from the pleasant and not receiving what is desired, as given in the discourse, are to be considered as the psychological aspect of affliction. Then the fivefold grasping of the five aggregates is stated as the doctrinal aspect. The Second Truth, the root cause of the present affliction, which exists in the form of desire, is broken down into its constituents for the better understanding of that cause. In the Third, the state of being redeemed from afflictions by regaining health is described, which is nothing but *Nibbāna*, the Supreme Bliss. In the Fourth Truth, the remedy to ameliorate the affliction is prescribed by way of the Noble Eightfold Path. It is quite clear that the theory of causality also applies to the analysis of suffering, the cause of suffering, the appeasement of suffering and the path leading to the appeasement of suffering.

The Therapeutic Approach

Buddhism when taken as a whole is therapeutic in character. It analyses causes and conditions of the present predicament of human existence and suggests remedial measures to be followed for the alleviation of it. Because of the scientific methodology followed by the Buddha in the first sermon, the Cambridge psychologist Thouless says that it is very much like a modern lecture on bacteriology. Wherein the disease, the cause of the disease by the multiplication of bacteria and viruses in the bloodstream and then the cure and destruction of the invading bacteria and viruses by injecting antibiotics and other medicinal substances to the bloodstream of the patient is explained.

The therapeutic approach is so fundamental to early Buddhism, Thouless does not hesitate to name it as a system of psychotherapy.[4] The Buddha's approach to suffering and its remedy was so rational and convincing that a later Indian philosopher, too, followed the same methodology of analysis in order to explain the cyclic existence of beings. He is none other than Patanjali who referring to the science of medicine drew the analogy of disease, the cause, the recovery and the cure emphasizes that Yoga philosophy is also divided into four sections. The cycle of existence is suffering, the cause of suffering is the union of *prakrti* and *purusa*. The termination of the union is release. Right vision is the means of release.

The commentator Buddhaghosa, too, elucidating the implications of the Four Noble Truths, the simile in question has also been drawn among other similes. For he says:

> "The truth of suffering is like a disease, the truth of origin is like the cause of the disease, the truth of cessation is like the curing of the disease and the truth of path is like the medicine."[5]

Assuredly, Buddhaghosa was influenced not by Patanjali, but by an earlier reference in the canon itself, where the imagery of healer and medicine has been drawn to illustrate the Buddha and the doctrine. There Pingiyani says to Karanapalin:

> "Just sir, as a clever physician might in a moment take away the sickness of one sick and ailing, grievously ill, even so, whenever one hears the

---

[4] Thouless Robert H.- *Christianity and Buddhism*, p. 5
[5] *Vis. XVI*, p. 87

master Gotama's dhamma, grief, lamentation, suffering, sorrow and despair vanish."[6] Thus the therapeutic approach is an appreciative quality particular to the doctrine preached by the Buddha.

Is Buddhism Pessimistic?

The word *'dukkha'* denotes and connotes the totality of our existence. However there are some writers, disturbed by the fact of *'dukkha'* being discussed as the First Noble Truth in Buddhism, incline to hold the wrong view that Buddhism is pessimistic in outlook from the very beginning.

What is pessimism? Pessimism is a gloomy view of life. A pessimist sees only the worst aspect of everything. He always anticipates defeat. Because of wrong notions haunting in his mind, he is afraid of facing the facts of life. Pessimism, being an inner check of free activity, overwhelms one with despair, frustration, inaction and inhibition. Contrary to the hopelessness, which characterises pessimism, optimism offers a bright view of life full of hope. The optimist is locked up in fool's paradise, in a utopia for the time being.

See the short and sharp sarcasm of the following two English epigrams on "The Optimist" and "The Difference":

> The optimist fell ten stories.
> At each window bar,

---

[6] *A. III*, p. 273

He shouted to his friends:
"All right so far."

'Twixt optimist and pessimist
The difference is droll
The optimist sees the doughnut
The pessimist sees the hole.

When he realises the fact of *'dukkha'*, which is woven into the very fabric of our existence, he is disappointed and depressed. When we come face to face not only with the world of experience, but also with our inner feelings, aspirations and proclivities, we are confronted with all sorts of problems. The non-recognition of the stark realities of life is indeed not a reason to ignore the facts of vicissitudes of life. Therefore Buddhism teaches us to understand things, as they really are *(yathābhūta)*. Since the Buddhist approach is neither pessimistic nor optimistic it advocates realism which lies between those two extremes. Besides, Buddhism does not stop at analysing the constituents of *'dukkha'*, on the contrary, it shows an antidote to overcome it.

The psychoanalyst Freud said that man is always suffering from an uncertainty, a fear expressed in terms of anxiety. This harrowing uneasiness of his mind overpowers his reason.

The existentialist philosopher Kierkegaard emphasised man's fear that torments him when he is confronted with life's problems. He named that mental tendency as 'anguish' and declared that it can only be relieved by transcendental faith in God. But two other existentialists, Heideggar and Jean Paul Sartre, totally denying the existence of God, said the honest encounter with dread and anguish is the only gateway to 'authentic' living.

Philosopher Kant was emphatic in stating that man is ever in a predicament. Yet nobody calls them pessimists. The concept of *'dukkha'* is to be considered as a correct philosophy of life. For he says:

> "I think that primitive Buddhism must be understood as a system of psychotherapy. Acceptance of Christian faith may of course also give relief from mental burdens but this is only incidental whereas the therapeutic aim of Buddhism is fundamental. This is why I think we can feel that many of the teachings of the Buddha are relevant to our needs in a way that would have been impossible to our grandfathers, because we have accepted and become used to the aim of psychotherapy".

All the Four Truths are connected to each other by way of causal relatedness. The right attitude to be developed towards suffering is explained in the Fourth Truth. The foremost position ascribed to right understanding in the path is significant in this regard. The understanding of the real nature of life helps individuals model their attitude to life for the betterment of this life here and the life after.

The commentator Buddhaghosa winding up his long discussion on suffering says:

> "It is impossible to tell it (all) without remainder, showing each kind of suffering, even for many eons. So the Blessed One said 'in short the five aggregates of clinging are suffering' in order to show concisely how all that suffering is present in any one of the five aggregates (as objects) of clinging. In the same way, that the taste of the

water in the whole ocean is to be found in a single drop of its water."[7]

🕮 🕮 🕮

Origin of Suffering

The Buddha explains to Acela Kassapa:

"Avoiding both the dead-ends of eternity-view and annihilation-view, the Tathagata teaches the Dhamma by the Middle Way: Conditioned by ignorance are the kamma-formations...... and so on. Thus is the origin of this mass of suffering."

-S., II, p. 19-21

---

[7] *Vis.* XVI, p. 60
   (This chapter is to be considered as a continuation of chapter 3)

Craving as Psychodynamic Thought and Narcissism

"The Buddha describes two types of craving, each of which has a counterpart in psychodynamic thought. The first, the craving for sense pleasures, we can grasp immediately......... The second, what the Buddha called the craving for *existence and nonexistence,* is what we would today call *narcissistic* craving: the thirst for a fixed image of self, as either something or as nothing. It is the craving for security wherever it can be found: in becoming or in death."

-Mark Epstein
Thoughts without a Thinker, p. 59

6. The Second Noble Truth: Cause of Suffering (dukkhasamudaya sacca)

The Second Noble Truth of the Four Noble Truths deals with the cause of suffering. The cause of suffering is none other than craving (*tanhā*). In the first discourse of the Buddha, while describing the Second Noble Truth, craving is explained with three epithets together with its three aspects, which cover the entire range of human suffering in the cycle of births and deaths. The brief description of craving given in the discourse runs thus: "And what is the cause of suffering? It is craving, which causes rebirth (*ponobhavikā*), is accompanied by delight and lust (*nandirāgasahagatā*), and finding pleasure in this or that (*tatra tatrābhinandinī*), namely, Craving for Sense Pleasures (*kāma-tanhā*), Craving for Being (that is, for continued existence) (*bhava-tanhā*), and Craving for Non-being (that is, for personal annihilation) (*vibhava-tanhā*)." [1]

English and Pali Synonyms for Craving

It is to be noted that craving (*tanhā*) in Buddhism includes all varieties of desire ranging from passionate lust or cupidity to subtle affection and attachment of any kind. Therefore the Pali word '*tanhā*', derived from √*trs* to be thirsty, has been rendered into English not only as 'craving', but also as 'desire', 'lust', 'greed', 'attachment', 'love', 'affection', 'passion', 'thirst', 'yearning' and the like

---

[1] *S.* IV, p. 420 ff. and *Vin.* I, 10 ff.

in different contexts. Just as in the first discourse, in the Dependent Origination, too, the word '*tanhā*' has been used to denote craving that causes grasping or clinging leading to repeated existence.

'*Tanhā*' is a very significant word in both Buddhist philosophy and psychology. It is charged with religious emotion and delineates the causal genesis of suffering and the psychological aspect of entire human behaviour. As the first of the three roots of evil, the word '*lobha*' or '*raga*' denotes craving, hatred *(dosa)* and delusion *(moha)* being the remaining two of the three roots of evil. The absence of which is the Supreme Bliss (*Nibbāna*). The different aspects of craving have been brought to light in the discourses. A wide variety of terms such as: '*kāma*' (sensual pleasure), '*chanda*' (desire), '*kamacchanda*' (desire for sensual pleasure), '*rāga*' (lust), '*rati*' (attachment), '*pema*' (love), '*sineha*' (affection), '*gedha*' (greed), '*nandi*' (delight), '*pipāsa*' (thirst), '*parilāha*' (consuming passion), '*mucchā*' (swoon), '*issā*' (envy), '*macchariya*' (avarice) are used.

The causal link between suffering and craving is a discovery of the Buddha, which led the Buddha to search for a way out of the conditioned relatedness of suffering and craving. As the Buddha has shown, when the cause of craving ceases to be, the resultant suffering ceases to be simultaneously.

Threefold Craving in Relation to Six Senses and Six Sense Objects

The complexity of threefold craving in the original classification has been described by multiplying the three into hundred and eight in relation to six senses, sense objects and past, present and future. In respect of one's eye, ear, nose, tongue, body and mind, and external objects of form, sound, smell, taste, contact and concepts, craving becomes twelvefold. In relation to threefold analysis of craving for sense pleasure, craving for being and craving for non-being, craving is counted as thirty-six, which again multiplied by three periods of time: past, present and future, thus making it hundred and eight (6+6=12x3=36x3=108).

Craving as a Multi-Significant Term in Buddhist Doctrine

In the *Sakkapañha-sutta* of the *Digha-nikaya,* all conflicts and confrontations in the world are traced to craving associated with the prolific tendency of the human mind. In the dialogue between the Buddha and Sakka, the Buddha traces the causal genesis of conflicts to envy and avarice rooted in things dear and not dear, which in turn based on desire *(chanda)* leading to initial application *(vicāra)* and proliferation of perception *(papañca saññā sankhā).* By nature craving springs up and thrives wherever it finds something delightful and pleasurable.[2]

---

[2] *D.* II, p. 276 ff.

Therefore the *Dhammapada* illustrates the nature of craving with apt similes:

> "Folk is enrapt in craving, is terrified like a captive hare. Therefore a monk who wishes his own passionlessness, should discard craving."[3]

> "Riches ruin the foolish but not those in quest of beyond. Through craving for riches the ignorant man ruins himself as if he were ruining others."[4]

> "From craving springs grief, from craving springs fear; for him who is wholly free from craving there is no grief, much less fear."[5]

In the same vein, endearment *(piya)*, affection *(pema)*, attachment *(rati)* and lust *(kāma)* have been mentioned as the root cause of grief and fear.[6]

Because of craving one clings on to pleasurable thoughts, therefore, "if in anyone the thirty-six streams of craving that rush towards pleasurable thoughts are strong, such deluded person, torrential thoughts of lust carry off."[7]

Inter-relatedness of craving and suffering is stated with emphasis:

---

[3] *Dhp.* 343
[4] *Dhp.* 335
[5] *Dhp.* 216
[6] *Dhp.* 212-215
[7] *Dhp.* 339

"Whosoever in the world overcomes this base unruly craving, from him sorrows fall away like water drops from a lotus leaf."[8]

"Just as a tree with roots unharmed and firm, though hewn down, sprouts again, even so, while latent craving is not rooted out, this sorrow springs up again and again." [9]

In the *Sunakkhatta-sutta*, craving has been compared to an arrow and ignorance to a poisonous humour. There the Buddha says that that arrow has been removed and the poisonous humour cured by Him. Continuing, the Buddha says that pursuing the sight of unsuitable forms with the eye, unsuitable sounds with the ear, unsuitable odours with the nose, unsuitable flavours with the tongue, unsuitable tangibles with the body or unsuitable mind objects with the mind enables lust to invade the mind. When the mind thus invaded by lust, suffering would follow. [10]

In the lively dialogue between the king Koravya and Elder Ratthapala found in the *Raṭṭhapala-sutta*, four statements summarising the doctrine have been explained to the king by Elder Ratthapala:

1. Life in the world is unstable, it is swept away (*upaniyati loko addhuvo*).
2. Life in the world has no shelter and no protector (*attāno loko anabhissaro*).

---

[8] *Dhp.* 336
[9] *Dhp.* 338
[10] *M.* II, p. 256

3. Life in the world has nothing of its own; one has to leave all and pass on *(assako loko sabbaṁ pahāya gamanīyam)*.
4. Life in the world is incomplete, insatiate, the slave of craving *(ūno loko atitto tanhādāso)*.

The fourth statement summarises how the entire world is enslaved by craving. Being overwhelmed by insatiate desire, man is always in pursuit of more. The unappeasable nature of craving is explained with an illustrative anecdote by the Elder.[11]

The Threefold Craving

The first, Craving for Sensual Pleasure is related to external objects of sense gratification. The attachment to visual, auditory, olfactory, gustatory and tactile objects of eye, ear, nose, tongue and body that we yearn for, and fanatically pursue, end up in real suffering. It is not because of the evil inherent in those objects, but because of the wrong attitude adopted towards perception. In order to illustrate the danger in sensual pleasure many shocking similes have been given in the discourses. The *Alagaddūpama-sutta* of the *Majjhima-nikaya*, describes how sensual pleasure provides little gratification, much suffering and much despair and how great is the danger inherent in them. Similes of the piece of meat, the grass torch, the pit of coals, dream, the borrowed goods, the tree laden with fruits, the slaughter house, the sword stake, and the snake head have been drawn.[12] To show the futility of the fivefold sensuality, the *Potaliya-sutta* draws the simile of a meatless bone given to a hungry

---

[11] *M.* II, pp. 68-72
[12] *M.* I, p. 133

dog waiting by a butcher's shop. The dog would not be able to appease its hunger by gnawing the meatless bone. Eventually it would reap weariness and disappointment.

The Buddha, recollecting His experience in sensual pleasures, said to Magandiya:

> "Formerly when I lived the household life, I enjoyed myself, provided and endowed with the five cords of sensual pleasure, namely: with forms cognizable by the eye, with sounds cognizable by the ear, with odours cognizable by the nose, with flavours cognizable by the tongue, and with tangibles cognizable by the body that are wished for, desired, agreeable and likable, connected with sensual desire and provocative of lust. I had three palaces, one for the rainy season, one for the winter, and one for the summer. I lived in the rains' palace for the four months of the rainy season, enjoying myself with musicians who were all female, and I did not go down to the lower palace. On a later occasion, having understood as they actually are the origin, disappearance, the gratification, the danger and the escape in the case of sensual pleasures, I abandoned craving for sensual pleasures, I removed craving for sensual pleasures and I abide without thirst, with a mind inwardly at peace. I see other beings who are not free from lust for sensual pleasures being devoured by craving for sensual pleasures, and I do not envy them, nor do I delight therein. Why is that? Because there is, Magandiya, a delight apart from sensual pleasures, apart from unwholesome states, which surpasses divine bliss.

> Since I take delight in that I do not envy what is inferior, nor do I delight therein."[13]

The hedonistic attitude to life depicted in the habit of seeking sensual enjoyment is one of the extremes as outlined in the first discourse, the "Turning of the Wheel of Law". It is termed as Self-Indulgence *(kāmasukhallikānuyoga)* which advocates the best of pleasures for the senses. Basing their argument on materialist view of life, some of the philosophers argued that as there is nothing surviving death, one should enjoy life by whatever means, as long as one lives.

Craving for being *(bhava-taṇhā)* is rooted in the belief of an immutable soul, an ego in one's body, which is termed as eternalism *(sassatavāda)*. According to eternalistic view, as soul is imprisoned in the body, one has to be born again and again to practise Holy Life, so that soul should get united forever with the universal soul *(paramatman)*. Fifty-five varieties of eternalist views are given in the *Brahmajala-sutta* of the *Dīgha-nikaya*.

Craving for non-being *(vibhava-tanhā)* is out-and-out nihilism, advocating pleasures of the flesh. Broadly speaking both Craving for Sensual Pleasures and Craving for Non-Being *(vibhava-tanhā)* are based on materialist view of life. According to both groups of theorists there is no permanent entity called soul, which is only a psycho-physical unit that does not survive death. Therefore they maintained that one should enjoy life by whatever means, as long as one lives. In *Brahmajāla-sutta* seven types of nihilist views have been outlined.

---

[13] *M.* I, pp. 505-6

Craving as the Origin of Personality and Suffering

Craving is the origin of personality. It is because of the threefold craving that personality originated. When the question of the origin of personality was put to Bhikkhuni Dhammadinnā by Visākha, she replied:

> "Friend Visakha, it is craving, which brings renewal of being, is accompanied by delight and lust, and seeking pleasure in this and that; that is, craving for sensual pleasures, craving for being, and craving for non-being. This is called origin of personality by the Blessed One."[14]

Her reply embodies what the Buddha said in His first discourse. In the same way venerable Sariputta addressing the monks in the *Sammadiṭṭhi-sutta* said that origin of suffering is threefold craving.[15]   In the *Salāyatanika-sutta*, how craving contributes to bodily and mental suffering is vividly described:

> "When one abides inflamed by lust, fettered, infatuated, contemplating gratification, then the five aggregates affected by clinging are built up for oneself in the future, and one's craving gives rise to renewed existence........ One's bodily and mental troubles increase, one's bodily and mental fevers increase and one experiences bodily and mental suffering."

---

[14] *M.* I, p. 299
[15] *M.* I, p. 48

The *sutta* states further that because of the ignorance of the real nature of the six senses, sixfold consciousness, sixfold contacts, and pleasant or painful or neither pleasant nor painful feelings, one is subjected to both bodily and mental suffering.[16] The *Chachakka-sutta* discussing the underlying tendencies, traces suffering to ignorance and craving.[17]

📖📖📖

No Craving, how can there be Grief or Fear?

> *"From craving is born grief,*
> *from craving is born fear.*
> *For one freed from craving*
> *there's no grief*
>   *-so how fear?"*

-Dhammapada, 216
Translated by Thanissaro Bhikkhu

---

[16] *M.* III, p. 287
[17] *M.* III. p. 285

Nibbāna as the Destruction of Lust, Hatred and Delusion

The wandering ascetic Jambukhadaka visited venerable Sariputta and asked:

> "'Nibbāna, Nibbāna!' is the saying friend Sariputta. Pray, tell me friend, what is Nibbāna?"

Venerable Sariputta replied:

> "The destruction of lust, the destruction hatred, the destruction of delusion, friend, is called Nibbāna."

-S. IV, p.251

7. *The Third Noble Truth: Cessation of Suffering (dukkhanirodha sacca)*

The Third Noble Truth is the Cessation of Suffering. In the first sermon, it is described as the cessation of craving without residue and with dispassion (*asesavirāganirodho*), giving up *(cāgo),* complete abandonment *(patinissaggo),* release *(mutti),* and non-attachment *(anālayo).* With reference to the Four Noble Truths, it is stated that the Buddha gained the knowledge that the First Noble Truth is to be comprehended fully *(pariññeyyaṁ),* and already comprehended it fully *(pariññātaṁ).* The Second is to be abandoned *(pahātabbaṁ),* and already abandoned *(pahīnaṁ);* the Third is to be realised *(sacchikātabbaṁ),* and already realised *(sacchikataṁ);* and the Fourth is to be developed *(bhāvetabbaṁ),* and already developed *(bhāvitaṁ).*

Nibbāna as the Cessation of Suffering

The cessation of suffering by destroying craving, the root cause, is the objective of Buddhist training which culminates in realisation of *Nibbāna*, the Supreme Bliss. In the brief introduction of the Third Noble Truth found in the first sermon, the total destruction of craving is emphasized with four terms of similar import, signifying the relation between craving and suffering. The uniqueness of the Buddhist approach lies in the fact of realising the transcendental truth, by each individually, with one's own personal effort. Hence rejecting the view of vicarious salvation, it asserts that dhamma is 'to be realised individually by the wise with their personal effort' *(paccattaṁ veditabbo viññūhi)*. As Buddhism does not maintain any kind of concept involving a theory of soul to be saved or almighty creator god who acts as saviour of suffering humanity, the cessation of suffering is to be achieved by practising the path enunciated by the Buddha.

Nibbāna is an ethical state to be reached in this life by ethical practice, which includes concentration and insight. However, the etymology of the word is described in different ways. Originally, in the canonical references it bears an affinity to blowing off *(nibbāyati)* and most certainly the implication is the blowing off of the three roots of evil: craving, ill-will and delusion. (Compare with *"nibbanti dhīrā yathā'yaṁ padīpo"*) Therefore it has been formed from √*vā* to blow, hence *nir* +√*vā* means blowing out. But later Pali etymologists seem to have preferred to derive the word from √*vr* to cover (*nir*+√*vr*), implying the going out of fire of defilements due to covering it up or by not feeding it with further fuel or by withdrawing the cause of its production.

The commentator Buddhaghosa gave the meaning 'dissociation from craving' to the word. His descriptive definition of the word brings out the nature of *Nibbāna* according to Theravada point of view. He says:

> "It is called disillusionment of vanity *(mada)*, on coming to it, all kinds of vanity, such as the vanity of conceit, and vanity of manhood, are disillusioned, undone, done away with. And it is called elimination of thirst, because on coming to it, all thirst for sense desires is eliminated and quenched. But it is called abolition of reliance

because on coming to it, reliance on five cords of sense desire is abolished. It is called the termination of the round, because on coming to it, the round of the three planes of existence is terminated. It is called destruction of craving, because on coming to it, craving is entirely destroyed, fades away and ceases. It is called *Nibbāna*, because it has gone away from *(nikkhanta)*, escaped from *(nissaṭa)*. It is dissociated from craving, which has acquired the common usage name 'fastening' *(vāna)*. Because by ensuring successive becoming, craving serves as a joining together, a binding together, a lacing together, of the four kinds of generation *(yoni)*, five destinies *(gati)*, seven stations of consciousness *(viññanaṭṭhiti)* and nine abodes of beings *(sattāvāsa)*."[1]

Elucidating the ethical perfection denoted by the word *Nibbāna*, venerable Ñānamoli states in his English translation of the *Visuddhimagga*[2]:

"The original literal meaning was probably 'extinction' of fire by ceasing to blow on it with bellows (a smith's fire for example). It seems to have been extended to extinction of fire by any means, for example, the going out of a lamp's flame *(nibbāyati-M. iii*, 245). By analogy it was extended to the extinction of greed etc., in the *Arahant*, with the resultant extinction of the five aggregates process on the Arahant's death (see *Iti.* 38). *Nibbāna* is not the extinction of self or of a living lasting being, such a mistaken opinion

---

[1] *Vis.* p. 293
[2] *The Path*, Footnote 72, p.319

being the Annihilation View (see e.g. *M. I,* 140, *S. iii,* 109)".

Evidently, the Buddhist meaning conveyed by the word is nothing but the extinction of three roots of evil.

Nibbāna as Indefinable in Terms of Logic and Reasoning

Nibbāna is an experience, which cannot be grasped in terms of logic and reasoning. Hence it is explicitly stated that it is beyond the range of logic *(a-takka-avacara=atakkāvacara),* which means that Nibbanic Bliss is not in the field of logic or a logical category that can be grasped with reason by employing the tools of logic. The expression, 'beyond the range of logic' delineates the place given by Buddhism to reason and logic in defining the highest religious truth in Buddhism.

The truths in Buddhism, as quoted above from the first sermon, are based on the experience the Buddha gained when He attained Enlightenment. The Buddha has shown that some of the truths cannot be communicated by language applying logical reasoning. The fact is obvious for several reasons.

During the time of the Buddha, there were some teachers who formulated and communicated their own teachings in terms of logic. They were known as rationalists and metaphysicians. They were concerned with the logical format of their theories, so that others should get convinced. Logic per se is concerned only with the logical consistency of a theory. Consequently, a theory may be logically sound with regard to forms and premises, but it may be factually wrong.   One can develop consistent theories having no correspondence whatsoever with empirical or transcendental truths. Thus any teacher who is conversant with the apparatus of logic can contrive a theory basing his arguments on logic, but at the same time misusing it to serve his purpose. Thus on logical proof, a theorist may argue that his theory alone is true, whereas others are false.

So much so, in the *Kālāma-sutta*, the Buddha's charter of free inquiry, four propositions have been given to illustrate the inadequacy of logic as a means of knowledge. According to the *Sutta*, a view is not to be accepted merely because of its:

i.   basic logical format *(takka-hetu)*
ii. merely on the view that seems rational *(naya-hetu)*
iii. reflecting on mere appearance *(ākāraparivitakka)*
iv. agreement   with   a   considered   view *(diṭṭhinijjhānakkhanti)*.

In the *Brahmajāla-sutta* two contemporary theories named as products of rational thinking and metaphysical speculation *(takkapariyāhataṁ   vīmaṁsānucaritaṁ)* have been rejected as unsatisfactory. Critizing this type of speculative philosophers, the *Suttanipata* says: "They say the two things: true and false, by employing logic on views." *(takkaṁ ca diṭṭhīsu pakappyitvā – saccaṁ musā'ti dvayadhamma āhu – Sn.* 886).

In the *Sandaka-sutta* the Buddhist attitude is clearly shown by dissecting the format of logic together with its outcome. One may arrive at a correct conclusion *(yathā)* either by a well-formulated argument *(sutakkita)* or by an ill-formulated argument *(dutakkita)*. In the same way

one may arrive at an incorrect conclusion *(aññathā)*
either by a well-formulated argument or by an ill-
formulated argument[3].

Therefore Buddhism is emphatic in asserting that the
logical reasoning is unsatisfactory as a means of
knowledge. This does not mean that Buddhist truths are
illogical and Buddhism is vehemently opposed to any
kind of logical reasoning. Buddhism is aware that
reasoning can be used in a proper way to get one's
statements of truth verified. Nevertheless, it is against the
view that logic alone is true as a valid means of
knowledge. Buddhism accepts that logical reasoning has
a limited value. Because it is stated in the canon that 'so
far as anything can be ascertained by reasoning, thou has
ascertained it' *(yāvatakaṁ .... pattabbaṁ anuppattaṁ
tayā...).*[4]

In saying that truths cannot be expressed by logic,
Buddhism maintains the insufficiency of language to
convey experience beyond empirical. Words by which
language is constituted, have been invented by man to
describe the facts of ordinary experience. The fable of
the Tortoise and the Fish illustrates the fact quite clearly.
Although the tortoise being amphibious tried his best to
explain land to the fish, because of the fact that its
experience is confined only to water, it was not in a
position to understand what is land. Also in fact, quite
often, a word may give rise to different ideas to different
persons in different contexts. Another feature of words is
they change their meaning from time to time. Then
words have to be considered as not reliable. Logic, which
uses words in the form of arguments, can suffer from

---

[3] *M.* I, p. 520
[4] *S. I*, p. 56

these defects. Hence the Buddha's emphasis is on knowledge based on experience.

Nibbāna in Negative Perspective

Because of these defects of language and logic, avoiding wrong conceptions that may occur, *Nibbāna* is explained in negative terms. In fact, the word *'Nibbāna'* and *'nirodha'*, the two most commonly used words to denote the Supreme Bliss, are negative in form. As explained earlier, *'Nibbāna'* being the extinction of the three roots of evil, *'nirodha'* is used to denote the absence of suffering. Buddhaghosa defining the word says:

> "The prefix *'ni'* denotes absence, and the word *'rodha'*, a prison *(ni-saddo abhāvaṁ, rodha-saddo ca carakaṁ dīpeti)*. Now the Third Truth is void of all destinies by rebirth, and so there is no constraint *(rodha)* of suffering here reckoned as the prison of the round of rebirth......... Or alternatively, it is called 'cessation of suffering' because it is a condition for the cessation of suffering consisting in non-arising."[5]

Together with the expression 'beyond the scope of logic' *(atakkāvacara)*, a host of other negative terms also have been used in the canon to denote *Nibbāna*. It is unborn *(ajāta)*, unoriginated *(abhūta)*, unmade *(akata)*, unconditioned *(asaṃkhata)*, difficult to be seen *(duddasa)*, difficult to be comprehended *(duranubodha)* and freedom from all bonds *(yogakkhema)*. As it is an experience beyond all conditional phenomena of empirical world, it is difficult to be expressed in ordinary

[5] *Vis.* p. 495

language, which is only an instrument of communicating our day to day mundane experience.

Nibbāna in Positive or Conventional Perspective

Positively speaking it is the highest happiness *(nibbānaṁ paramaṁ sukhaṁ)*. In contradiction to worldly happiness it is the permanent *(nicca)*, eternal *(dhuva)*, happy *(sukha)* and pleasant *(subha)* state experienced by destroying all defilements. Therefore in conventional terminology, it is the supreme happiness one can think of.

In a conversation between Elder Sariputta and Elder Udayi, the nature of this happiness is elucidated by Elder Sariputta.

The Elder said:

> "This *Nibbāna* is, friend, happiness. This *Nibbāna* is, friend, happiness."

Then the Elder Udayi asked:

> "But how could herein be happiness, if herein nothing to experience with senses."

The Elder Sariputta replied:

> "The absence of experience through senses, friend, itself is happiness."

Then the Elder proceeds on to explain how the five
strands of sense desire and the happiness arising
therefrom, is called sensuous happiness and also how the
happiness experienced in each jhanic state which is not
sensuous, becomes better than the former one, thus
climaxing in *Nibbāna*.[6]

Sopādisesa and *Anupādisesa Nibbāna*

Nibbanic Bliss is attained in this very life by destroying
the defilements, which bind a being to the cycle of
existence. Buddhism ensures that its ideal state, the
ultimate goal can be attained in this life. In respect of
realisation *Nibbāna* is twofold, *Sopādisesa* and
Anupādisesa.

It is stated in the *Itivuttaka* by the Buddha:

> "Herein, O monks, a monk is an Arahant, one
> who has destroyed the defilements, who has lived
> the life, done what was to be done, laid aside the
> burden, who has attained his goal, who has
> destroyed the fetters of existence, who, rightly
> understanding, is delivered. His five sense organs
> still remain, and as he was not devoid of them he
> undergoes the pleasant and unpleasant
> experiences. That destruction of his attachment,
> hatred and delusion is called the Element of
> *Nibbāna* with substratum still remaining"

---

6   *" Kiṁ pana ettha āvuso sukhaṁ yadi ettha natthi*
     vedayitaṁ'ti? Etadeva khvattha āvuso sukhaṁ yadi ettha
     natthi vedayitaṁ'ti"—A. IV, pp.414-5

Referring to the other, it is stated that the attainment of *Nibbāna* of an Arahant, after his demise leaving his substratum behind, is *Anupādisesa Nibbāna* [7].

📖📖📖

Nibbāna in Positive Terms

"Monks, there is a not-born, a not-become, a not-made, non-compounded. Monks, if that unborn, not-become, not-made, non-compounded were not, there would be apparent no escape from this here that is born, become, made, compounded."

-Udana, p.80-1

---

[7] *Itivuttaka* p.38

Road Map to Nibbāna

The Buddha addressing the monks said:

> "There is a Middle Path for the abandoning of craving and hatred, giving vision, giving knowledge, which leads to peace, to direct knowledge, to enlightenment, to Nibbāna. And what is that Middle Path? It is just this Noble Eightfold Path."

-Dhammadāyāda-sutta, M. I, p. 16
MLDB. p. 100

8. The Fourth Noble Truth: Middle Path (majjhimā paṭipadā)

The Middle Path is to be followed for the elimination of suffering. The Path is called Middle because it lies between the two extreme paths of self-indulgence *(kāmasukhallikanu-yoga)* and self-mortification *(attakilamathānu-yoga)*, which had been practised by the Buddha prior to His Enlightenment. The futility of the two paths of practice for the realization of truth led the Buddha-aspirant to reason out a new path for the purpose of achieving the desired end. The Middle Path or via media stands as the Fourth Truth of the Four Noble Truths and it is the antidote to suffering.

Between these two practices, the more popular method of practice among the brahmins and other ascetics in India in the 6th century B. C. was self-mortification amounting to self-torture, inflicted by oneself, on one's own body. The practice being based on eternalistic view of life *(sassatavāda)*, penance was considered essential to get the soul released from the body-prison, enabling it to unite eternally with the universal soul. But the materialistic view *(ucchedavāda)* on the other hand, advocating sensual gratification at any cost and by any means, encouraged the pursuit of sensual pleasure. The materialists argued that soul is only a psycho-physical unit born of parents and does not survive death. Hence one has to enjoy life through whatever means as long as one lives. The Buddha from experience challenged the efficacy of these two extreme views for realization and laid bare their intrinsic incompatibility as well as inconsistency.

The Path enunciated by the Buddha is the prescription for the ills of existence. It is by this Fourth Truth that craving which binds one to cyclic existence and ever present in life, is to be destroyed. It is a set of practices, which has been practised by the Buddhas and the disciples in the past and rediscovered by the Buddha Gotama after a very long interval. [1] When it is called 'path' metaphorically, it is to be traversed by prospective disciples who wish to put an end to suffering. It ensures ethical and moral behaviour of the practitioner and leads him to liberation from suffering. It enhances the culture and development of one's three avenues of action: body, speech and mind for the betterment of oneself and other beings; ultimately leading one to perfection.

The Noble Eightfold Path *(ariyo aṭṭhangiko maggo)*

The Noble Eightfold Path, otherwise named as the Middle Path *(majjhimā paṭipadā),* consists of eight factors. It is to be noted that although it is called path, it is not to be taken as a gradual path having a series of steps. The factors of the Path are inter-related and to be practised simultaneously. Those factors are mutually inclusive and mutually supportive. The Path is, of course, described in terms of three aggregates consisting of morality *(sīla)*, concentration *(samādhi)* and wisdom *(paññā)*, but does not mean that those three aggregates are included in the Noble Eightfold Path. It is to be noted that the Noble Eightfold Path is included by the three aggregates of morality, concentration and wisdom. The question of the Noble Eightfold Path's position in relation to three

---

[1] *K.S.II,* p. 74

aggregates has been asked by Visākha from nun Dhammadinnā:

> "Lady, are the three aggregates included in the Noble Eightfold Path or is the Noble Eightfold Path included in the three aggregates?"

The bhikkhuni replied:

> "The three aggregates are not included by the Noble Eightfold Path, friend Visākha, but the Noble Eightfold Path is included by the three aggregates."[2]

As to how it is included in the three aggregates of practice is shown below.

The Noble Eightfold Path and Three Aggregates

1.	Right Understanding	*(sammā diṭṭhi)*
2.	Right Thought	*(sammā sankappa)*
3.	Right Speech	*(sammā vācā)*
4.	Right Action	*(sammā kammanta)*
5.	Right Livelihood	*(sammā ājiva)*
6.	Right Effort	*(sammā vāyāma)*
7.	Right Mindfulness	*(sammā sati)*
8.	Right Concentration	*(sammā samādhi)*

The three factors, Right Speech, Right Action and Right Livelihood are included in the aggregate of morality. The last three, Right Effort, Right Mindfulness and Right Concentration are included in the aggregate of concentration. The first two factors, Right Understanding and Right Thought, are in the aggregate of wisdom.

---

[2] *M. I,* pp. 301-302

Right Understanding is sometimes translated into English as Right View. It is explained as the knowledge of the Four Noble Truths: Suffering, Cause of Suffering, Cessation of Suffering and Noble Eightfold Path. The entire *Sammādiṭṭhi–sutta* of the *Majjhima-nikaya* is devoted to the explanation of Right Understanding. The *sutta* was delivered by Thera Sariputta to a group of monks who wanted to have thorough understanding of the subject. Primarily there are two, external and internal, factors conducive to Right Understanding. They are:

1.   Hearing from others *(paratoghosa)* and
2.   Thoughtful reflection *(yonisomanasikāra)*.

The hearing from others may include knowing from other sources of information as well. When one comes to know the dhamma by any source of information, he is asked to reflect thoughtfully what he came to know. The exercise of thoughtful reflection leads one to understanding. The information of dhamma one receives is the food for thought which one has to subject to careful scrutiny and analysis. It is the intellectual grasp of what one has come to know through any means of knowledge. It amounts to the understanding of the real nature of the phenomenal existence.

It is stated that when one understands that body, sensation, perception, mental formations and consciousness are impermanent, he is led to Right Understanding. Then he is convinced of the efficacy of moral causation dealing with actions of moral significance and their results *(kammassakata-ñāna)* together with the knowledge of correct understanding of the Four Noble Truths *(saccānulomika-ñāna)*. The knowledge of this stage is called 'knowing accordingly' *(anubodha)*, because the understanding at this stage is still mundane Right Understanding *(lokiya-sammādiṭṭhi)* and not yet free from defilements. The penetrative knowledge of Right Understanding appears only when one realises one or the other of the four stages of sanctification: Stream-winning, Once-returning, Non-returning and Arahanthood. The knowledge of Right Understanding at those stages is called supra-mundane or transcendental Right Understanding *(lokuttara-sammādiṭṭhi)*. The mundane Right Understanding is developed by ordinary worldlings *(puthujjana)* but the supra-mundane Right Understanding comes under the purview of Noble Ones *(ariyapuggala)*. This stage of understanding is at the highest level and unshakable.

Right Thought is defined as having mainly three constituents: renunciation or giving up of sensual enjoyment *(nekkhamma-sankappa)*; developing thoughts of loving kindness and goodwill without any kind of anger and hatred *(avyāpāda-sankappa);* and practising amity and concord, abstaining from violence *(avihimsā-sankappa)*.

The thoughts must be free from lust and craving which hanker after pleasures of the senses. Buddhism eschews any kind of violence. Hence is the development of loving kindness and non-violence towards all living beings. This shows that in addition to the practice of some of the other factors of the Path, Right Thought becomes meaningful in the context of society.

Right Speech is the practice of correct speech, which amounts to avoiding lying *(musavāda)* and adhering to truth; to abstaining from tale-bearing or back-biting *(pisunāvācā)* which paves the path for dissension and disunity. Promoting social harmony, one must abstain from using harsh language while cultivating courteous and gentle words in communication; and should avoid irresponsible, vain talk such as gossiping and speak only what is meaningful and conducive to one's and others' welfare.

Right Action deals with abstinence of three kinds of bodily misconduct: taking life, theft and misappropriation, and sexual misconduct. The mundane Right Action produces wholesome worldly results whereas the practice of transcendental Right Action, avoiding those misbehaviours completely with pure mind intent upon the Path, is contributory to deliverance. Right Action guarantees the fundamental human rights of right to live, right to possess and right to maintain sexual relations within the confines of legally permitted boundary.

Women under the protection of father, mother, brother, sister or relatives, married women, women under the ban of the king, engaged women and women who are the temporary wives of others are mentioned as the women to be avoided in sexual intercourse.

Right Livelihood is to reject wrong kinds of living and live by right means of livelihood. Wrong livelihood means gaining a living by earning wealth by devising ways and means detrimental to sentient beings. In this connection, usually five kinds of trade are mentioned in the text. They are: trading in arms *(satthavanijjā)*, human beings *(sattavanijjā)*, flesh *(maṁsavanijjā)*, intoxicating drinks *(majjavanijjā)* and poisons *(visavanijjā)*.

Right Effort is the Four Great Efforts *(cattaro sammappadhānā)*. It enjoins the putting forth effort consciously in four ways: to prevent the arising of unwholesome thoughts that have not yet arisen; to abandon unwholesome thoughts that have already arisen; to develop wholesome thoughts that have not yet arisen; and to maintain wholesome thoughts that have already arisen by one who practises the Path of Emancipation.

Right Mindfulness deals with the four kinds of contemplation: contemplation of the body *(kāyānupassanā)*, of sensation *(vedanānupassanā)*, of mind *(cittānupassanā)* and of mind-objects *(dhammānupassanā)*. It is said in the *Satipaṭṭhāna-sutta* "the disciple dwells in contemplation of the body, of sensation, of mind and mind-objects, ardent, clearly conscious and attentive, putting away worldly greed and grief". This refers to the setting up of mindfulness in four ways. The practice as given in the discourse leads to purity, to the overcoming of sorrow and lamentation, to the end of pain and grief, to the entering upon the correct path and the realisation of *Nibbāna*.

Right Concentration is the attainment of meditative absorptions *(jhāna)*. There are five hindrances that obstruct the path of deliverance. Through meditative absorptions one can overcome the five hindrances: desire for sensual pleasure *(kamacchanda)*, illwill *(vyāpāda)*, sloth and torpor *(thīna-middha)*, restlessness and worry *(uddhacca-kukkucca)* and sceptical doubt *(vicikicchā)*. When one attains the first meditative absorption, these hindrances are destroyed by the psychic factors of the meditative absorption *(jhānanga)*.

Thus desire for sensual pleasure is destroyed by one-pointedness of the mind *(ekaggatā)*, illwill by joy *(pīti)*, sloth and torpor by initial application *(vitakka)*, restlessness and worry by happiness *(sukha)* and sceptical doubt by sustained application *(vicāra)*. In the *Anguttara-nikaya* the nature of five hindrances is illustrated with an alluring simile. Desire for sensual pleasure is like coloured water; illwill is compared to boiling water; sloth and torpor to water covered with moss and weeds; restlessness and worry to water tossed and turbulent due to wind; and sceptical doubt to muddy water.[3] Just as in any one of these instances one cannot see one's reflection, the mind overwhelmed by the hindrances will not penetrate things as they really are.

The Middle Path in Relation to Social Welfare

Buddhist ethics has been sadly misunderstood by many to the extent of saying that it is only a set of abstentions without any positive cultivation of ethical practice. Here we propose to examine this misconception in relation to the Middle Path taught in Buddhism and how it is relevant to weal and welfare of society.

Buddhist Social Ethics

Basically, the three factors of the path; Right Thought, Right Speech and Right Action, which come under the aggregate of morality as explained earlier have a direct influence on society. As one can clearly see, social ethics in Buddhism is practicable only in relation to society. These ethical practices bind individual and society together. In other words, ethical and moral behaviour prescribed in these factors becomes meaningful only in the context of society. Also to a considerable extent, social concern is implicit even in the other two

---

[3] *A. V*, p.193

aggregates, concentration and wisdom, of the path of Buddhist practice.

Let us take Right Thought, the second factor of the Noble Eightfold Path. When taken as a whole, it is giving up the pursuit of sensual enjoyment, developing thoughts of loving kindness and goodwill without an iota of resentment, anger or illwill while practising amity and concord free from violence and cruelty which are instrumental in harming others.[4]   Right Thought is a factor to be developed and put into practice in relation to society for the good and happiness of oneself and society.

Therefore the social implication of this factor is quite clear from the fact that renunciation of personal enjoyment, giving up of thoughts of illwill and abstinence from violence have to be practised while one lives in society.   Hence when he develops and practises the right kind of thoughts free from evil thoughts harmful to other beings, it is needless to say that society is benefited by his moral conduct.   Positively, when he develops love, goodwill and amity, his attitude towards fellow human beings falls into proper focus and he contributes in his personal capacity to the course of welfare of society.

Now, let us take the third factor, Right Speech. As described in many a discourse, he who practises Right Speech gives up false speech and refrains from false speech; he speaks the truth (*saccavādi*), is reliable (*saccasandho*), firm (*theto*) and as he is trustworthy (*paccayika*) he does not deceive people.

---

[4]   *D.* II, p. 312

He gives up back-biting and abstains from back-biting. If he has heard anything here, he will not tell it elsewhere in order to cause dissension among the people or if he had heard something there, he will not tell it to the people here in order to cause dissension among the people. Thus he becomes either a conciliator of enemies (*bhinnānaṁ vā sandhātā*) or a supporter of the friendly (*sahitānaṁ vā anuppadātā*). He rejoices in unity (*samaggārāmo*), delights in unity (*samaggarato*), finds happiness in unity (*samagganandi*) and speaks words that promote unity (*samaggakaranaṁ vaccaṁ bhāsitā hoti*) among men.

He gives up harsh speech and refrains from harsh speech. He will speak words that are gentle (nela), pleasant to hear (*kannasukha*), kind (*pemanīya*), heart-stirring (*hadayangama*), polite (*pori*), agreeable to many people (*bahujanakanta*), pleasing to many people (*bahujanamanāpa*).

He gives up gossiping and refrains from gossiping. He speaks at the proper time (*kālavādī*), he speaks the truth (*bhūtavādī*), he speaks what is useful (*atthavādī*), he speaks what is righteous (*dhammavādī*), he speaks what is conducive to restrain (*vinayavādī*), he speaks words that are worth remembering (*nidhānavatiṁ vācaṁ*), well-grounded (*sāpadesaṁ*), purposeful (*pariyantavatiṁ*) and profitable (*atthasaṁhitaṁ*).[5]

Here what is noticeable is, both the negative and positive aspects of Right Speech are described in relation to society, ensuring both one's own welfare as well as the welfare of society.

---

[5] *A*. V, p. 205

As described earlier, the practice of the other two factors of the path, Right Action and Right Livelihood, too, are beneficial in two ways. The practitioner becomes morally good and instrumental in bringing about social well being.[6]

📖📖📖

The Eightfold Path Leads to Nibbāna

"This Eightfold Path is the way leading to the cessation of consciousness."

-S., III, p. 61

---

[6] Gnanarama P. Ven. – *An Approach to Buddhist Social Philosophy*. pp. 4-5

Dependent Origination as the Middle Path

The Buddha elucidates the right view to venerable Kaccayana:

> "This world Kaccayana, usually rests on two things: on existence and non-existence. He, who with right insight sees uprising of the world as it really is, does not hold with the non-existence of the world. But he, who with right insight sees the passing away of the world as it really is, does not hold with the existence of the world. Grasping after systems, imprisoned by dogmas is this world, Kaccayana, for the most part. And the man, who does not go after that system grasping, that mental standpoint, that dogmatic bias, does not grasp at it, does not take up his stand upon it. .... 'Everything exists' is one extreme, 'nothing exists' is the other extreme. Not approaching either extreme, Tathagata teaches a doctrine by the middle, namely; through ignorance conditioned are the kamma-formations (and so on)."

-S. II, p. 17

9. *The Buddhist Theory of Dependent Origination (paṭiccasamuppāda)*

T he Buddhist theory of Dependent Origination is one of the fundamental teachings of Buddhism. To begin with, the Buddha after His Enlightenment, as recorded in the *Mahavagga-pali,* reflected on the causal genesis of phenomena by way of twelve links dependent origination from beginning to the end and end to the beginning. Furthermore, the three verses given in the text as the first utterance of the Buddha after the Enlightenment also summarise the theory as most fundamental to Enlightenment. It is stated in the verses given after the progressive and retrogressive cogitation on the twelve links of the causal genesis, when the meditative brahmana discerns the causes and the destruction of the causes, all his doubts begin to vanish and he shines as the sun in the sky routing the forces of Evil One. It is also important to note that in this connection, when Assaji, the fifth of the five first converts, was asked what the teaching of the Buddha was, confessing that he did not know much of the doctrine, he revealed the Dependent Origination as the essence of the Buddha's doctrine. The stanza he uttered has been considered as a doctrinal summary of Buddhism throughout the ages:

> "Those things proceed from a cause, of these the Truth-finder has told the cause,
> And that which is their stopping, the great recluse has such a doctrine."

(Ye dhammā hetuppabhavā tesaṁ hetu tathagato āha yesaṁ ca yo nirodho evaṁ vādi mahasamaṇo) [1]

The Theory as the Central Doctrine of Buddhism

The theory is so fundamental to Buddhism it can be considered as the central doctrine in Buddhist thought. Its relation to other principal doctrines taught in Buddhism is too obvious to be ignored. The Four Noble Truths have been elaborated on the basis of conditional relativity: suffering, cause of suffering, cessation of suffering and path leading to the cessation of suffering. In the same way the three characteristics of existence have been established on causal interdependency of impermanence, suffering and non-substantiality. The Buddhist teaching of *kamma* and rebirth is also explained on the basis of moral causation of cause and effect. All phenomena, whether they are internal or external, are causally conditioned *(saṁkhata)*. Hence the Buddha's assertion:

> "He who sees the Dependent Origination sees the dhamma, he who sees the dhamma sees the Dependent Origination."

> *(yo paṭiccasamuppādaṁ passati so dhammaṁ passati yo dhammaṁ passati so paṭiccasamuppādaṁ passati.)* [2]

---

[1]   *Vin.* I, p. 41
[2]   *M.* I, p. 191

When the Buddha preached the first sermon, the 'Turning of the Wheel of Law', it is stated that the *dhamma eye* which is spotless and pure, referred to in the *sutta* as "whatever is in the nature of arising (due to causes and conditions) is in the nature of ceasing to be" *(yaṁ kiṁ ci samudayadhammaṁ sabbaṁ taṁ nirodhadhammaṁ)*, appeared in Kondañña. Here the spotless and pure *dhamma eye* is explained as the first stage of Sainthood, the attainment of which is marked with the understanding of causal genesis of phenomena.

It is not a subjective category imposed by the mind on phenomena. It is objective and it denotes the plurality of conditional relations or relative coexistence of causes and conditions in genesis of phenomena. Its objective characteristic is emphasised with the terms objectivity *(tathatā)*, necessity *(avitathatā)*, invariability *(anaññatā)*, and conditionality *(idappaccayatā)*. [3]

Its objectivity of causal interdependence is stressed throughout as a fact. Causal sequence is an independent occurrence of phenomena and it is free from any subjective intervention by the mind. It is stated that whether Tathagatas arise or not this order *(dhātu)*, namely, the fixed nature of phenomena *(dhammaṭṭhitatā)*, regular pattern of phenomena *(dhammaniyāmatā)*, or conditionality *(idappaccayatā)*, exists in the world. This the Tathagata discovers and comprehends; having discovered and comprehended it, He points it out, teaches it, lays it down, establishes, reveals, analyses, clarifies it and says: "Look!" [4]

---

[3] *S.* II, p. 26
[4] *S.* II, pp. 25-6

Synonymous Terms Used in Pali and in English

The theory of Dependent Origination has been rendered into English in numerous ways following the different terms given in Pali. Acariya Buddhaghosa in the *Visuddhimagga* gives *'paccaya'*, *'hetu'*, *kārana*, *'nidāna'*, *'sambhava'*, *'pabhava'* as synonymous terms. But he says although the words are different, the meaning is the same.[5]   In English, however, the theory is introduced as Interdependent Origination or Dependent Origination; sometimes as Causal Genesis or Conditional Genesis; and as Causality or Theory of Causes and Effect. 'Theory of Causation' presumably stands for *'hetuphala-vāda'* and Conditionality or relativity for *'idappaccayatā'*. The *paccaya* theory developed in Abhidhamma is introduced as the theory of conditional relations.

The Causal Relativity as a General Rule

Dependent Origination or causal relativity is a feature common to both physical and psychical spheres. Hence the correlation of cause and effect has been brought to light by two basic formulae, abstract and concrete, which can be readily applied to every phenomenon whether internal or external. The abstract formula establishes the link between cause and effect with a one-to-one correlation:

---

[5] *Vis.* II, p. 532

"Whenever this is present, this is (also) present
Whenever this is absent, this is (also) absent"
*(imasmiṁ sati idaṁ hoti
imasmiṁ asati idaṁ na hoti)* [6]

The concrete formula given in many places in the canon is specific with regard to the causal genesis, interdependence and cessation and illustrates how the theory is applicable to every phenomenon that arises and ceases to be in the world of experience. It is the world of change.

"From the arising of this, this arises
From the cessation of this, this ceases to be"
*(imassa uppādā idaṁ uppajjati
imassanirodhā idaṁ nirujjhati)* [7].

On the basis of the theory, Buddhism repudiates pre-Buddhist theories of accidentalism, determinism, eternalism, materialism, fatalism as well as the theories of creation and soul pertaining to man and his destiny. In the same vein, later Hindu theories are refuted by the Buddhist theory of Dependent Origination. Such as Saktivāda of Pūrva mīmansā which posits the view that cause is a kind of force. Satkāranavāda or Vivartavāda of Vedanta upholds the view that cause is the manifestation of Being. Satkāryavāda of Sānkhya emphasises the effect is contained in the cause; and Asatkāryavāda or Ārambhavāda of Nyāya-Vaisheshika professes the effect as a new beginning and that it is not contained in the cause.

---

[6] *Ud.* p. 2
[7] *Ud.* p. 2; *M.* I, 263; *S.* II, P. 70

The Chain of Causation

The theory of causation or the formula of Dependent
Origination with twelve links in progressive order is an
application of the causal relativity to suffering and
repeated existence in the cycle of births and deaths. In
other words, it deals with a causal account of the factors
that operate behind human suffering and the
psychological reasons, which cause one to be born again
and again in numerous spheres of births unfolding links
of previous life, present life and the life immediately after
this life. What is significant is, the chain while rejecting a
metaphysical causal agency or a First Cause, explains the
whole process of suffering and repeated existence
empirically in terms of causal interdependence. It runs
thus:

1-2	*avijjā*	*paccayā*	*saṁkhārā*
2-3	*saṁkhāra*	*paccayā*	*viññānaṁ*
3-4	*viññāṇa*	*paccayā*	*nāmarūpaṁ*
4-5	*nāmarūpa*	*paccayā*	*salāyatanaṁ*
5-6	*salāyatana*	*paccayā*	*phasso*
6-7	*phassa*	*paccayā*	*vedanā*
7-8	*vedanā*	*paccayā*	*taṇhā*
8-9	*taṇhā*	*paccayā*	*upādānaṁ*
9-10	*upādāna*	*paccayā*	*bhavo*
10-11	*bhava*	*paccayā*	*jāti*
11-12	*jāti*	*paccayā*	*jarā-maraṇa-soka-parideve-dukkha-domanassa upāyāsā sambhavan'ti.*

1-2   Through Ignorance conditioned are the *Kamma*-formations.

2-3   Through the *Kamma*-formations conditioned is Consciousness.

3-4   Through Consciousness conditioned are Mentality and Corporeality.

4-5   Through Mentality and Corporeality conditioned are the Six Sense-bases.

5-6   Through Six Sense-bases conditioned is Sense-impression.

6-7   Through Sense-impression conditioned is Feeling.

7-8   Through Feeling conditioned is Craving.

8-9   Through Craving conditioned is Clinging.

9-10   Through Clinging conditioned is Rebecoming.

10-11 Through Rebecoming conditioned is Rebirth.

11-12 Through Rebirth conditioned are Decay, Death, Sorrow, Lamentation, Pain, Grief and Despair. Thus arises the whole mass of suffering.

According to the retrogressive order, with the fading away of Ignorance, *Kamma*-formations become extinguished. And through the extinction of *Kamma*-formations, Consciousness, Mentality and Corporeality, Six Sense-bases, Sense-impression, Feeling, Craving, Clinging, Rebecoming, and Rebirth are extinguished respectively. Through the extinction of Rebirth; Decay, Death, Sorrow, Lamentation, Pain, Grief and Despair cease to be. Thus extinguishes the whole mass of suffering.

The Fact that Ignorance is not the First Cause

In explaining the causal interdependence of suffering and rebirth, the Buddha has employed several methods other than the twelve-link formula popular in Buddhist circles.

As discussed in the *Visuddhimagga*[8] the seventh to twelfth links are highlighted in some instances while some other occasions, the retrogressive order from eighth to first. Besides these, there is yet another method of explanation beginning from third to twelfth is found in the *Sanyutta-nikaya*. The theory of *paccaya* found in the *Paṭṭhāna* is an elaboration of the theory of dependent origination with twenty-four conditional relations. As vindicated by different methods of presentation, ignorance is not to be considered as the first cause. It has been expressly stated that the first beginning of ignorance is not known and that there is no particular point of time to show that ignorance has arisen from that point of time, but what is discernible is that ignorance is also subject to the law of causal conditionality.[9]

Inductive Inference and the Theory of Causation

According to the canonical references the Buddhist theory of causation is an outcome of normal perception on observable data and proved to be true by paranormal perception. The relative interdependence of phenomena as an observable fact has been explained by the elder Sariputta in the *Nalakalapaniya-sutta* of the *Sanyutta-nikaya,* with the simile of two sheaves of reeds kept erect with each other's support. When one is taken away the other can no longer stand erect.[10] Herein, elder Sariputta explains the relative nature of causation, where resultant effect ceases to exist when the preceding cause

---

[8] *Vis.* Chap. XVII
[9] *A.* V. p. 113
[10] *S.* II, p. 112 ff.

ceases to exist. In other words the simile illustrates the fact that the chain is no more when relativity is no more.

□□□

By not Comprehending the Dependent Origination........

When once the Buddha was staying among the Kurus, the venerable Ananda approached him and said:

"It is wonderful, Lord, that while Dependent Origination is so deep and looks so deep, to me it seems perfectly clear."

"Do not speak like that, Ananda. For this Dependent Origination is deep and looks deep too. It is not from awakening to this Dhamma, Ananda, from not penetrating it, that this generation, become tangled like a ball of thread, covered as with blight, twisted up like grass-rope, cannot overpass the sorrowful state, the bad bourn, the abyss, the circling on cyclic existence."

-Mahānidāna-sutta
D.,II, 55

The Smallest Unit of the Universe

The smallest unit of the universe called sahassi cûlanikâ lokadhâtu, i. e. the Thousandfold Minor world system. As far as these suns and moons revolve, shining and shedding their light in space, so far extends the thousandfold universe. In it are thousands of suns, thousands of moons,....... thousands of Jambudîpas, thousands of Aparagoyânas,............. subtle material worlds (rūpaloka) or the worlds of higher spirits or gods as being associated with the material worlds or galaxies.

-A., I, p.227

10. Abodes of Beings and World Systems as Described in Buddhism

As described in the canonical texts Buddhas appear in the world in order to preach what is suffering and the cessation of suffering. In illustration of the fact of suffering in the cycle of births and deaths by being subjected to repeated existence, incidentally, abodes where the beings are born are explained with considerable detail.

Saṁsāra or the cycle of births and deaths, although some have wrongly taken to mean abodes or planes where the beings are born, it does not mean planes of existence, it is the nature of being born in these abodes repeatedly. These abodes of beings have been described by some Western scholars under the generic title Buddhist cosmology. According to Buddhist description there are thirty-one abodes in all, where beings are born in their wanderings in *saṁsāra*.

Abodes of Beings

Four abodes of unhappiness in the sensual sphere *(kāmadugati):*

1. Purgatory *(Niraya)*

    Where beings are born because of their evil *kamma*. These are not to be understood as hells where beings are subjected to suffering eternally. But are more or less like purgatories, the places of punishment and torture where one's evil *kamma* is atoned. Because of the terrible ordeals one is subjected to in these purgatories they are partly compared to Hades, the abode of the dead in Greek mythology. Upon the exhaustion of the evil *kamma* of the being he is born in another abode. There are eight major purgatories: *Sañjīva, Kālasutta, Sanghāta, Roruva, Mahāroruva, Tapana, Patāpa* and *Avīci*. Among them the last named is the most fearful one. Altogether one hundred and thirty-six purgatories are mentioned in the texts including the subdivisions of the major ones.

2.   Animal kingdom *(Tiracchāna-yoni)*

Where beings are born as animals because of their evil deeds. But upon the exhaustion of evil *kamma,* they are born in some other abodes. This is not a particular plane or abode as such, but it is the very world of ours where the animals of different kinds live.

3.   World of Departed Ones *(Peta-yoni)*

There is no particular plane for them. They live everywhere on this earth undergoing the effects of evil *kamma* they have done in previous existence. Sometimes the word *'peta'* is rendered as 'ghost' or 'spirit'. There are four kinds of petas as described in the *Milindapañha: Vantāsika* who feed on vomit, *Khuppipāsino* who are always hungry and thirsty, *Nijjhāmatanhikā* who are consumed by craving, and *Paradattūpajīvi* who live on the gifts of others. The *Petavatthu* describes vividly the suffering they undergo with deformed physical bodies due to evil deeds they had done in their previous lives. The last named petas are able to enjoy the merits transferred to them by the living friends and relatives and pass on to better abodes of happiness. Among different kinds of petas, *kumbhanda* and *pisāca* are also mentioned.

4. Demon world *(asura-yoni)*

This is the abode or the plane of *asura* demons. They are also described as unhappy beings destined to undergo consequences of their evil deeds. Another kind of *asura* who has some divine powers is mentioned in the texts as the enemy of gods.

Seven Abodes of Happiness in the Sensual sphere *(kāmasugati)*

1. The Human World *(manussaloka)*

The human world is said to be the best of the worlds to be born in. Being a human one is able to fulfil the perfections to be a Buddha.

2. The heaven of the Four Guardian Deities *(catummahārājika)*

This is the plane of the four guardian deities called Kuvera or Vessavana, Virūlha, Virūpakkha and Dhataraṭṭha. They have their own followers. Their glory and magnanimity is described in the *Āṭānāṭiya-sutta* of the *Digha-nikaya*. Dhataraṭṭha being the head of *gandabbas*, another kind of semi-divine beings, rules over the eastern direction. Virūlha, the head of *kumbhandas* is the guardian of the South. The head of *nāgas*, Virūpakkha, is the guardian of the West and Kuvera or Vessavana, head of *yakkhas*, North.

3. The Heaven of the Thirty-three Gods *(tāvatiṁsa)*

    The chief of this heaven is famous Sakka who is
    always out to help the virtuous fallen into trouble.
    Sakka is said to have been born there with his thirty-
    two companions as a result of social service they
    volunteered to do in a previous birth.

4. The Heaven of the Yāma Devas *(yāma)*

    The gods of this heaven live in divine luxury
    experiencing no pains.

5. The Heaven of the Tusita Devas *(tusita)*

    This is also a happy place. It is the heaven of delight.
    The Future-Buddha, the Buddha Metteyya is in this
    heaven awaiting the right opportunity to be born in
    the human world.

6. The Heaven of the Nimmānarati gods *(nimmānarati)*

    The gods of this heaven delight in mansions created
    by themselves.

7. The Heaven of the Paranimmitavasavatti gods
    (paranimmitavasavatti)

    The gods of this heaven delight in the mansions
    created by other gods.

The four woeful spheres, human world and six heavenly
spheres are collectively known as eleven sensual spheres
(kāmaloka).

The Spheres of Form *(rūpaloka)*

1. The Sphere of Brahma's retinue *(brahmapārisajja)*
2. The Sphere of Brahma's ministers *(brahmapurohita)*
3. The Sphere of the Great Brahmas *(mahābrahma)*
4. The Sphere of Minor Lustre *(parittābha)*
5. The Sphere of Infinite Lustre *(appamānābha)*
6. The Sphere of the Radiant Brahmas *(ābhassara)*
7. The Sphere of the Brahmas of Minor Aura *(parittasubha)*
8. The Sphere of the Brahmas of Infinite Aura *(appamānasubha)*
9. The Sphere of the Brahmas of Steady Aura *(subhakinha)*
10. The Sphere of the Brahmas of Great Reward *(vehapphala)*
11. The Sphere of the Mindless Beings *(asaññasatta)*
12. The Durable Sphere *(aviha)*
13. The Serene Sphere *(atappa)*
14. The Beautiful Sphere *(sudassa)*
15. The Clear-Sighted Sphere *(sudassi)*
16. The Highest Sphere *(akaniṭṭha)*

   1 - 3 are first *jhāna* spheres.
   4 - 6 are second *jhāna* spheres
   7 - 9 are third *jhāna* spheres
   10 - 16 are fourth *jhāna* spheres
   12 - 16 are named Pure abodes *(suddhāvasa)*

Formless Spheres *(arūpaloka)*

1. The Sphere of Infinite Space *(ākāsānañcāyatana)*
2. The Sphere of Infinite Consciousness *(viññānañcāyatana)*
3. The Sphere of Nothingness *(ākiñcaññāyatana)*

4. The Sphere of Neither Perception nor Non-Perception
    (n'eva saññānāsaññāyatana)

World Systems

From the Buddhist point of view, the universe is
constituted of three world systems. But it is to be noted
that there is no specific word for universe in Buddhism.
The word 'loka' denotes both 'world' and 'universe'. The
words, *'lokadhātu'* and *'cakkavāla'* stand for world
systems. According to Buddhism there are innumerable
world systems in the universe. Therefore in this context,
as Prof. K.N. Jayatilleke maintained, the word *'loka'*
means the 'world of space'. The smallest unit of the
universe is termed 'Thousand-fold Minor World-System'
(sahassi cūlanikā loka-dhātu). This is how it is
explained: "As far as these suns and moons revolve,
shining and shedding their light in space, so far extends
the thousand-fold universe. In it are thousands of suns,
thousands of moons,....... thousands of Jumbudipas,
thousands of Aparagoyānas, thousands of Uttarakurus,
thousands of Pubbavidehas............" [1] The description,
however, illustrates the fact that in this Thousand-fold
World System, although it is the smallest unit, there are
innumerable planets in this system which have been
inhabited by beings of some form or other.

Then we are told of another world system which is
named as 'Twice-a-thousand Middling World System'
(dvisahassi majjhimikā loka dhātu).

---

[1] *A.* I, p. 227; *A.* IV, p. 59

In the Buddhist texts we come across further descriptions on 'Hundred Thousand-fold World Systems' *(sata-sahassi lokadhātu).*[2]

📖📖📖

Looking at the Universe in a Different Way

The Buddha addressing Rohitassa Devaputta said:

> *"Neither do I say, friend; that by not having got to the end of the universe is the end of suffering to be accomplished. It is in this fathom long body, friend, with its impressions and ideas that, I declare, lies the universe, the cause of the universe, the cessation of the universe and the course of action that leads to the cessation of the universe."*

> *-A. II, p. 62*

---

[2] *M.* III, p. 101

Freedom of Investigation

When Upali the Jain householder expressed his strong desire to be a Buddhist follower, the Buddha requests him:

> *"Investigate thoroughly, householder. It is good for such well known people like you to investigate thoroughly."*

-Upali-sutta, M. I, p. 379
MLDB. p. 484

11. Freedom, Free Will and Responsibility in Buddhist Perspective

F reedom, Free Will and Responsibility are concepts discussed essentially in modern Western philosophy. In justifying the philosophical approach of religious teachings, therefore, these themes in philosophy are applied and discussed often in relation to world religions, with subtle arguments and elaborate descriptions, which necessitate a clear understanding of the concepts as interpreted in Western philosophy.

Philosophical Exposition of the Terms

Freedom can be defined in numerous ways; power or condition of acting without compulsion, liberty, rights, independence, exception, immunity, unrestricted use, privilege, political rights and the like. Individualism and socialism may differ from each other in defining its contents. Having close affinity with the word liberty, the term freedom is applied in political sphere to bring out numerous implications pertinent to humans and institutions. The English philosopher John Locke (1532-1704) being an empiricist among other philosophers and theologians, held the view that an individual is possessed of some natural rights of freedom to develop one's own potentialities. Philosophically speaking the concept has negative and positive denotations. Negatively, according to Thomas Hobbes (1588-1679), the English philosopher, freedom is the absence of constraints and it is the silence of the law. But positively, freedom is a challenge that is only met by personal transformation and it is defined as a condition of liberation from social and cultural forces that are recognized as impediments to full realisation. So much so, Hegel (1770-1831) the German philosopher, asserted that freedom is to be achieved by social transformation.

As discussed in philosophy the concept of Free Will is also ambiguous and interpretative in the same way. The problem is the extent of freedom of will that we experience in our everyday consciousness of ourselves as agents of actions. How far are we free? Is there a limitation to free will? As a 'social animal' has not man been bound by social norms? Has not human nature itself imposed some constraints to man's actions? How far are our actions free? Or are they conditioned or determined?

As psychologists say parental training, advertising, mass media, 'brainwashing', simply circumstance and environment play prominent roles in determining the actions of an individual, he being a victim of circumstances and his environment he is not personally responsible for his actions. He has been conditioned to act in that particular way.

Certainly, in Buddhism too, five laws that influence the world and individual have been discussed covering a wider range of complex phenomena found in the world: physical, biological, psychological, natural and kammic. But it does not mean that there is no free will. It is argued by theologians like St. Augustine (354-430) that as God himself is sole causal agent in the entire universe, therefore, an individual's actions are predetermined by God's prior decision and acknowledgement. The contradictory nature of these theistic and deterministic arguments has been shown by Gunapala Dharmasiri in his *"A Buddhist Critique of the Christian Concept of God"*.

William James (1842-1910), the American psychologist and philosopher, arguing on the dilemma of determinism brought forward two arguments to refute determinism. The feeling of remorse after performing an action and the expression of regret for not doing it otherwise by some individuals, have no meaning had they not the possibility of choosing an alternative action. This vindicates the fact that there is free will since an optional course of action could have been perpetrated by them. Again, he argued that attribution of responsibility and meting out punishment to an offender is meaningless if he has been predetermined to do that act, because nobody condemns or punishes the determined material objects taking them to be free agents. If we punish offenders because of conditional factors influencing us, punishment has no moral significance since it becomes meaningful only in the context of free will and responsibility. The problems of freedom, free will and responsibility entail a long and exhaustive discussion of the subjects involving intricate philosophical, religious and social arguments as discussed by philosophers, theologians and sociologists.

Responsibility is socially as well as personally perceived as accountability. Hence one's failure to discharge a responsibility renders one liable to be punished and censured. Presumably in social ethics, the extent of responsibility is enlarged to embrace a wider circle other than oneself. Moral responsibility of any action is of religious significance, which is much emphasised in Buddhism.

Buddhism on Freedom, Free Will and Responsibility

These concepts are not discussed in Buddhism in equal or identical Pali terms. But it is to be understood that they are found distinctly in a coherent manner by different terms in numerous discourses in the canonical texts. Many are the philosophical arguments adduced to both validate and invalidate these concepts in relation to world religions. As modern philosophy covers a wider range in its discussions of these relative concepts, it is advisable to confine our definitions of the terms particularly to the sphere of Buddhist teaching. Then it is not difficult to find out the Buddhist attitude to the concepts of freedom, free will and responsibility through the analysis of the related themes of the doctrine.

Evidently, it is only when freedom is present, then can we speak of free will and responsibility. But obviously they have been interpreted to uphold any monotheistic or natural deterministic theory pertaining to religious beliefs. Also on the other hand, these concepts supply a sound basis to refute the monotheistic and deterministic theories. Arguments to prove or disprove their position within a given religious context have virtually rendered the terms more or less meaningless.

Hence in order to avoid ambiguity of their application it is plausible for us to define them in Buddhist perspective for the clear understanding of the Buddhist standpoint. In Buddhism, however, these concepts become meaningful in the context of self-perfection and self-realisation of the highest good envisaged in Buddhism. As Buddhism propounds an ethical theory of its own, together with positive recommendations to be adhered to, for the betterment of individual and society, these concepts are to be discussed within that frame of reference. Hence, freedom is to be understood as freedom to choose any moral or immoral action whether good or evil, free will as purposive willing, and responsibility as one's responsibility for the retributive effect of that action.

Purposive will is not accidental. As man has the power of selecting any moral action, will is manifested as one's ability to select any kind of moral or immoral action. As Buddhism does not propose a causal determinism, it stresses the fact of restraining the mind with the aid of the mind[1] and not to be under the sway of the mind but to put the mind under one's sway.[2]   Mind is the forerunner and thoughts arise in the mind,[3] but if the mind is bereft of the ability of controlling it, the individual is to be ever in the cycle of existence being bound by the causal nexus. Then eventually, *Nibbāna*, the goal propounded as beyond causal interdependence would be meaningless.

Buddhist ethics, both individual and social, become meaningful and expressive only when freedom and free will are guaranteed for the achievement of the ultimate goal, which lies beyond the causal conditioning of empirical phenomena.   As there is no invisible, supernatural agent wielding his power over human destiny, Buddhism ascribes the responsibility of moulding

---

[1] "*Cetasā cittaṁ abhiniggaṇhitabbaṁ abhisantāpetabbaṁ*" – *M.* I, pp. 120-1

[2] "*Cittaṁ vasaṁ vattati, na cittassa vasena vattatī*" –*M.* I, p.214

[3] "*manopubbaṁgamā dhammā*" – *Dhp.* 1

one's own destiny to the individual himself in no uncertain terms. For it is said in the *Dhammapada*:

"Oneself indeed is one's saviour, for what other saviour there be? With oneself well restrained one obtains a saviour difficult to find."

(Attā hi attano nātho – ko hi nātho paro siyā attanā'va sudantena – nātham labhati dullabham)[4]

Therefore rejecting the idea of a saviour and the saved Buddhism accepts freedom in respect of individual's moral behaviour making free will or freedom of choice and the corresponding responsibility as essential constituents of the path of realisation. In the same vein, Buddhism emphasises the facts of free will and moral responsibility stating that evil done by oneself would grind him just as a diamond grind a hard gem:

"By oneself alone is evil done; it is self-born, it is self-caused. The evil grinds the unwise as a diamond grinds a hard gem."

(Attanā'va katam pāpam – attajam attasambhavam Abhimanthati dummedham – vajiram v'asmamayam manim)[5]

Yet there is another stanza in the *Dhammapada* where the personal responsibility is highlighted in respect of moral action with the total rejection of an external agency for one's purification to arrive at the final goal.

---

[4]   *Dhp. 160*
[5]   *Dhp. 161*

"By oneself, indeed, is evil done; by oneself is one defiled. By oneself is evil left undone; by oneself, indeed, is one purified. Purity and impurity depend on oneself. No one purifies another."

(Attanā'va katam pāpam – attanā samkilissati
attanā akatam pāpam – attanā'va visujjhati
suddhi asuddhi paccattam – nāñño aññam
visodhaye)[6]

For the most part, the Buddhist teaching under discussion is contrasted more explicitly in delineating the weltanschauung of Makkhali Gosāla who lived in the 6th Century B.C. in India.

He is stated to have denied freedom, free will and responsibility with assertive terms such as *'natthi attakāro'* (nothing is done by oneself), *'natthi parakāro'* (nothing is done by others), *'natthi purisakāro'* (nothing is done by individual), *'natthi balo'* (no power), *'natthi viriyam'* (no energy), *'natthi purisathāmo'* (no personal strength), *'natthi purisaparakkamo'* (no personal endeavour).[7] He is said to have propounded *akiriyavāda,* the theory that denies the retribution of moral action thereby rejecting the personal responsibility of any action.[8]

On the other hand Buddhism preaches *kiriyavāda* professing moral responsibility of actions. In the *Apaṇṇaka-sutta* of the *Majjhima-nikaya, kiriyavāda* is introduced as a directly opposite theory (*ujuvipaccanikavāda*) to *akiriyavāda.* The discourse

---

[6]   *Dhp.* 165
[7]   *D.* I, p.53
[8]   *A.* I, p. 286

explains it further to convince the fact that the acceptance of the retributive efficacy of moral action is right understanding (*sammā diṭṭhi*), cherishing such thoughts is right thought (*sammā sankappa*) and speaking in accordance with the view is right speech (*sammā vācā*).

There is an interesting episode in the *Anguttara-nikaya*, where a brahmin who visited the Buddha denying free will on the part of oneself (*attakāra*) and others (*parakāra*). The Buddha then asked him how could he say so when he himself resolved to approach the Buddha and go away afterwards from Him. The Buddha in this connection explained to him six factors that contribute to free will, which can be considered as an empirical illustration of the fact of free will on the part of human beings without any specific reference to moral significance of purposive willing:

a) The element of initiative (*ārambha-dhātu*)

b) The element of origination (*nikkama-dhātu*)

c) The element of endeavour (*parakkama-dhātu*)

d) The element of steadiness (*thāma-dhātu*)

e) The element of immobility (*ṭhiti-dhātu*)

f) The element of volitional effort (*upakkama-dhātu*)[9]

---

[9] *A.* III, p. 337

The Buddha explained to him that these stages of willing are present in actions committed with free will and in subsequent responsibility of an action.

📖📖📖

Free Will and Determinism

"Doctrines of free will, positive appeals and moral exhortations to man prove absurdly futile in the face of any kind of determinism."

-Gunapala Dharmasiri
A Buddhist Critique of the Christian Concept of God, p.121

In Appreciation of Psychological Dimension in Buddhism

Psychologist William James was impressed with the psychological sophistication of Buddhism and predicted that it would be a major influence on Western psychology. While lecturing at Harvard in the early 1900s, James suddenly stopped when he recognised a visiting Buddhist monk from Sri Lanka in his audience.

"Take my chair," he is reported to have said.

"You are better equipped to lecture on psychology than I. This is the psychology everybody will be studying twenty-five years from now."

As Mark Epstein points out, James was one of the first to appreciate the psychological dimension of Buddhist thought.

> *-This incident is quoted by Mark Epstein in his "Thoughts without a Thinker", p.1, from Rick Fields' "How the Swans Came to the Lake: A Narrative History of Buddhism in America", p. 135.*

12. *Mind, its Nature and Function as Described in Buddhism*

Mind and its behaviour loom large in the Buddhist analysis of the individual. Cyclic existence which causes him to suffer now here and now there, until he gains release from it, is described in relation to the individual's mind and its improper function due to defiling unwholesome thoughts. Until the bonds by which he is bound to the cycle of births and deaths are torn apart through the purification of his mind, he will ever be in the cycle being subjected to suffering in numerous states of births. Hence, in the Buddhist scheme of morality leading to Supreme Bliss, mind plays a prominent role and the entire teaching of the Buddha can be termed as a system of psychoanalysis. Because of the tendency of analysing the mind and its functions in minute details Buddhism's psychological and ethical nature is more real than apparent.

What is Mind?

In the fundamental analysis of the individual into mind and form *(nāmarūpa)*, mind *(nāma)* refers to mind and other mental factors. The classification of the individual into five factors as form *(rūpa)*, sensation *(vedanā)*, perception *(saññā)*, mental formations *(saṁkhāra)* and consciousness *(viññāṇa)* is somewhat exhaustive and there the consciousness is mind while sensation, perception and mental formations are mental factors related to the functions of the mind. There is yet another classification where mental functions are classified in accordance with the sense faculties. In this classification of the individual into twelve faculties, eye *(cakkhu)*, ear *(sota)*, nose *(ghāna)*, tongue *(jivhā)*, body *(kāya)* and mind *(mana)*, there are six kinds of consciousness by way of their relationship to sense faculties. Hence mind becomes sixfold thus making the classification twelvefold together with eye consciousness, ear consciousness, nose consciousness, tongue consciousness, body consciousness and mind consciousness.

The Nature and Function of the Mind

Very many functions of the mind are recorded in the canon revealing its nature and function in different contexts. The mind's active and passive characteristics are brought to light in these references of the canon:

- It gives pleasure, propitiates and convinces *(ārādheti)*[1].

- It stretches forth, holds out, takes up, exerts, strains and vigorously applies in relation to its objects *(pagganhāti)*[2].

- It disposes, collects, brings together, heaps up, gathers, arranges, focuses and concentrates in numerous ways *(upasaṁharati)*[3].

- It bends, directs and applies *(namati)*[4].

---

[1] *S. II*, p.107
[2] *S. V*, p. 9
[3] *S. V*, pp. 213-216
[4] *S. I*, p. 137

- It springs forward, jumps onto, takes to and rejoices in its object *(pakkhandati, pasīdati, santiṭṭhati)*[5].

- It calms down and quietens *(passambhati)*[6].

- It agitates, disturbs, crushes, harasses and upsets an individual *(matheti)*[7].

- It shakes, unsettles, wavers and is in doubt *(vikampate)*[8].

- It holds back, obstructs, restrains, forbids *(nivāreti)*[9].

- It can strike, kill, destroy and beat down *(pahaññati)*[10].

- It aspires, longs for, prays for and intends *(panidahati)*[11].

- It clings to and gets bound up with its objects *(sajjati, gayhati, bajjati)*[12].

- It defiles, corrupts and tarnishes *(vyāsiñcati)*[13].

- It is drawn to, feels attached to, is inclined towards and indulges in its object *(adhimuccati)*[14].

---

[5] *S. I,* p. 98
[6] *S. V.* p. 33
[7] *S. IV,* p. 210
[8] *S. IV,* p. 71
[9] *S. I,* p. 7
[10] *S. IV,* p. 73
[11] *S. I,* p. 133
[12] *S. II,* p. 198
[13] *S. IV,* p. 178
[14] *S. V,* pp. 409-410

According to the foregoing definitions of the multi-faceted nature and function of the mind, it is quite clear that Buddhism recognises three functions of it:

1. affective
2. conative
3. cognitive

The affective aspect of the mind refers to the function of feeling that mind engages in. The conative function of the mind is acting, willing, striving and desiring and the cognitive aspect deals with the functions of knowing, believing, reasoning and perceiving. As these functions of the mind are not separable and detectable individually due to simultaneous action and interaction, the mental process becomes complicated, involved and complex.

The words popularly used for mind are *'citta'*, *'mana'*, *'viññāna'*, *'manasa'* and *'hadaya'*. Out of these, in the Pali canonical texts, the first three are often used to denote the mind. *'citta'* is from √cit - to think, *'mana'* as well as *'manasa'* is from √man - to think and *'viññāna'* is from √ñā - to know. *'Hadaya'* is heart; as the heart is considered the seat of the mind, consciousness or mind is also understood by the word *'hadaya'*. However, the three terms, *'citta'*, *'mana'* and *'viññāna'*, are described as synonymous[15]. Mind's functions of feeling, perceiving, conation and cognition are laid bare in many instances. It includes all sensory, perceptive, rational and subjective aspects of mind. In early Buddhism, all the aspects of mind are discussed in psychological, moral and naturalistic perspective. There is an attempt in Pali to bring out different functions of it with a number of verbs

---

[15] *S. II*. p. 94

coined from √ñā - to know. Thus to denote the function of knowing many verbal forms have been used:

Jānāti	knows
Vijānāti	knows with discrimination
Sanjānāti	recognizes
Pajānāti	knows with wisdom
Parijānāti	knows comprehensively
Abhijānāti	knows with extra sensory perception
Ājānāti	learns or grasps
Paṭijānāti	admits or approves

The *Dhammapada* on the Mind

Buddhism does not contribute to the view that mind can exist without physical support. It 'lies in the body cave' *(guhāsayaṁ)*. Illustrating the nature, function and the importance of restraining the mind, the *Dhammapada* also states:

> "Faring far, wandering alone, bodiless, lying in (body) cave, is mind. Those who subdue it are freed from the bond of *Māra*."[16]

The whole of the *Citta-vagga* of the *Dhammapada* is devoted to the explanation of the nature, function and the significant place it occupies in individuality. "Mind is flickering, fickle, difficult to guard and control"[17]. "Like a fish that is drawn from its watery abode and thrown upon land, even so does this mind flutter"[18]. "Mind is

---

[16]   *Dhp. 37*
[17]   *Dhp. 33*
[18]   *Dhp. 34*

hard to check, swift, flits wherever it listeth"[19]. "Mind is very hard to perceive, extremely subtle"[20]. "Mind is the forerunner of (all evil and good) mental states. Mind is chief; mind made are they"[21].

Mind is Conditional and Relative

In the Upanishads, mind has been interpreted to mean soul and called *'nirāsraya vijñāna'*. Generally in Western thought, too, mind is taken to mean soul. But it is to be emphasised that according to Buddhism, it is neither a soul nor a soul substance. Buddhist psychology found in the discourses of the Buddha and the analysis found in the later *Abhidhamma* treatises is a psychology without a 'psyche'. The fact of its conditional nature is stressed throughout the Buddhist scriptures.

There is a specific instance in the *Mahātaṇhāsankhaya-sutta* where the Buddha refuted the view that the same consciousness wanders from life to life experiencing the results of good and bad actions that one performed. When the venerable Sāti who held this view was asked by the Buddha to explain his view of consciousness and the relationship between the consciousness and one's actions, he replied:

> "Venerable sir, it is that which speaks, feels and experiences here and there the result of good and bad actions."

Then the Buddha said:

---

[19] *Dhp. 35*
[20] *Dhp. 36*
[21] *Dhp. 1, 2.*

> "Misguided man, to whom have you ever known
> me to teach the *dhamma* in that way? Misguided
> man, many discourses have I not stated
> consciousness to be dependently arisen, since
> without a condition there is no origination of
> consciousness? But you, misguided man, have
> misrepresented us by your wrong grasp and
> injured yourself and stored up much demerit; for
> this will lead to your harm and suffering for a
> long time."

Afterwards when the Buddha questioned the monks to
know whether they have correctly grasped the nature of
causal interdependence of consciousness, the monks
replied:

> "In many discourses the Blessed One has stated
> consciousness to be dependently arisen, since
> without a condition there is no origination of
> consciousness."[22]

The Classification of Mind in the *Abhidhamma*

Since mind occupies the pre-eminent place in the
Buddhist course of training of culturing the mind, in
Abhidhamma, mind has been classified into eighty-nine
varieties in accordance with the planes of existence:

I.   Fifty-four kinds of Consciousness pertaining to
      the sensuous sphere *(kāmāvacara)*.

---

[22] *M. I,* p. 258.

II.   Fifteen kinds of Consciousness pertaining to the sphere of forms *(rūpāvacara)*.

III.   Twelve kinds of Consciousness pertaining to the formless sphere *(arūpāvacara)*.

IV.   Eight kinds of Supra-Mundane Consciousness *(lokuttara)*.

Abhidhamma prefers to use the term *'citta'* for mind or consciousness, which usually deals with the subjective aspect of mind. This classification brings to light that the purpose behind the classification is purely moral. It is in conformity with the Buddhist theory of thirty-one planes of existence, which is sometimes introduced by some Western scholars as Buddhist cosmology. There is yet another importance of the classification; it brings into focus the Buddhist teaching on *kamma,* rebirth, meditative absorptions and the realisation of *Nibbāna* as the Supreme Bliss.

📖📖📖

Nature of the Mind

"Quivering, wavering,
hard to guard,
to hold in check:
the mind.
The sage makes it straight-
like a fletcher,
the shaft of an arrow."

-Dhammapada, 33
Translated by Thanissaro Bhikkhu

Universals and Particulars

Border guard stopped the horseman at the border and told him that horses were not allowed in.

Horseman:	"Horses refer to the universal, right? The 'horseness of all the horses'?"
Guard:	"Yeh."
Horseman:	"Now my animal is a white horse, which is a particular horse."
Guard:	"Obviously."
Horseman:	"So when this says 'horse', it means the universal, yes?"
Guard:	"I'll grant you that."
Horseman:	"You would agree that the universal and the particular are not the same, wouldn't you?"
Guard	"I am forced to agree with you there."

So, the horseman rode across the border on his horse.

-Kung-Sun Lung
White Horse Discourse
Ancient Philosophy for Beginners, p, 120

13. Authority and Logic in Buddhism

The place that authority and logic occupy in Buddhism can be understood by reviewing instances where they are discussed individually as well as in relation to other Buddhist concepts in the canonical texts. Evidently, these two apparatus of knowing and arriving at the truth particularly occupy a significant place in scriptural dialogues in connection with the quest for correct philosophy of life and the feasibility of religious life advocated therein. Indeed, authority in this context is not any kind of temporal authority possessing power or right to exert control or command, but in a religious and philosophical sense, it is the dependable and reliable religious authority and the source of religious and philosophical information, on which one should rely. Logic being the science of reasoning by formal methods focusing its attention to declarative sentences, which are used for the making of assertions, claims to find truth. Here we have to confine ourselves to finding its validity as a tool to arrive at religious truths. Therefore when taken together the place of both authority and logic occupy in Buddhism as valid means of knowledge come under the purview of the present discussion.

In pre-Buddhist India, the problem of authority was connected with traditionalists who were named as 'anussavikā' while logic was often related to metaphysicians or rationalists known as 'takki vīmaṁsī'. As both of these groups were outside the pale of Buddhism, in the discourses their views are often discussed side by side together with other unorthodox views. Here the Buddha distinguishes a third group of recluses and brahmins, who having directly known the *dhamma* for themselves among things not heard before, claim the fundamentals of holy life after having reached the consummation and perfection of direct knowledge. The Buddha identifies himself with this group of recluses and brahmins.[1]

The *Kālāma-Sutta* on Authority and Logic

The Traditionalists took the Vedas as authoritative because of the belief that Vedas had been revealed to the seers of old. As the Buddha points out those Brahmin seers namely: Aṭṭka, Vāmaka, Vāmadeva, Vessāmitta, Yamataggi, Angirasa, Bhāradvāja, Vāseṭṭha, Kassapa and Bhagu were the creators, the human composers of the hymns, whom the brahmins believed to have been divinely inspired[2]. So the Vedas were considered revealed and hence authentic *(suti)*. Thus originates the concept of revelation *(anussava)*. With some other corresponding assumptions revelation becomes sixfold:

1. Revelation *(anussava)*
2. Authority of tradition *(paramparā)*
3. Authority of hearsay *(itikira)*
4. Authority of sacred texts *(piṭakasampadā)*
5. Authority ascribed on the consideration of the competence of a person *(bhabbarūpatā)*
6. Authority attributed to a recluse considering that he is one's own teacher *(samaṇo no garu)*

---

[1]   *M.* II, p. 211
[2]   *M.* II, p. 169

Since all these six premises have been accepted as authentic by way of recognizing the sacred position ascribed to them, they are collectively called authority. Logic presumably takes its stand on reasoning as a means of religious and philosophical knowledge, which relies on:

1.   Basic logical format of a theory *(takka hetu)*
2.   View that seems rational *(naya hetu)*
3.   Reflection on mere appearance *(ākāraparivitakka)*
4.   Agreement with or approval of a considered view *(diṭṭhi nijjhānakkhanti)*

All these ten premises are discussed in the famous *Kālāma-sutta,* and the *sutta* further states that they are to be scrutinized with reference to greed, hatred and delusion, the three roots of evil[3].

The Buddhist Criticism of Authority and Logic

Buddhism expounds that both of these criteria are inadequate as means of knowledge because together with corresponding issues of these major premises they are ambiguous in their application. As shown by the Buddha in His reply to Kāpāṭika in the *Canki-sutta*:

1. Faith *(saddhā)*
2. Approval or inclination *(ruci)*
3. Revelation *(anussava)*

---

[3]   *A.* II, p. 191.

4. Reflection   on   mere   appearance
   (ākāraparivitakka)
5. Agreement with or approval of a considered view
   (diṭṭhi nijjhānakkhanti) may either be empty
   (rittaṁ), void (tucchaṁ) and false (musā) or
   factual (būtaṁ), true (taccbaṁ) and not
   otherwise (anaññatbā)

Presumably, the first two are emotive while the third is
blind acceptance. The last two hinge on logical
reasoning, speculation and sophistry free from any moral
implication. In fact the term logic is used more or less in
the sense of logic, sophistry and philosophical
speculation, thus the above five cover both authority and
logic under our discussion. The faith by which the
authority is attributed to the Vedas has been shown as
baseless faith (amūlikā saddbā) and brahmins who hold
on to the authority of the Vedas are compared to a file of
blind men, the first or the middle or the last could not
see. This faith is contrasted with 'faith supported by
reason, rooted in vision and firm' (ākāravati saddbā
dassanamūlikā daḷbā) which is the faith approved in
Buddhism[4]. In the Apaṇṇaka-sutta the Buddha questions
the brahmins of Sālā who visited the Buddha, whether
there is any teacher agreeable to them in whom they
have acquired faith supported by reason[5].

The foregoing five premises have been discussed in
several places to show their intrinsic incompatibility as
well as insufficiency in arriving at the truth. Once in a
friendly discussion among the elders Musila, Saviṭṭha,
Nārada and Ananda; the elder Saviṭṭha asked Musila
whether he (Musila) has the knowledge apart from these

[4]   M. I, p. 320
[5]   M. I, p. 401

five premises that decay-and-death is conditioned by birth. Then he replied that he saw and he knew that decay-and-death is conditioned by birth. And then the links of the dependent origination were traced in reverse order up to ignorance to show that he saw and knew them without any assistance from those five premises whatsoever[6]. There is another instance when the Buddha, addressing the monks, posed the question:

> "Is there, monks, any method other than these five assumptions, by following which, a monk affirms insight thus: ended is birth, lived is the noble life, done is the task, for life in these conditions there is no hereafter?"

Then on the request of monks, the Buddha explained how one should be aware of one's own visual, auditory, olfactory, gustatory and tactile sensations and evaluate them in terms of three roots of evil; greed, hatred and ignorance and recognize the non-existence of those qualities in oneself. The Buddha emphasizes the fact that it is the method of seeing things apart from the aforementioned five premises. It is nothing but seeing things with eye of wisdom leading to insight.[7]

With reference to the intrinsic ambiguity of these five premises, the *Canki-sutta* elaborates further that a premise may be:

1. Well accepted by faith or not well accepted by faith *(susaddahitaṁ / dusaddahitaṁ)*.
2. Well approved of or not well approved of *(surucitaṁ / durucitaṁ)*.

---

[6] S. II, p. 15 ff
[7] S. IV, p. 138

3. Transmitted well by oral tradition or not transmitted well by oral tradition *(svanussutaṁ / duvanussutaṁ)*.
4. Reasoned out well or not reasoned out well *(suparivitakkaṁ / duparivitakkaṁ)*.
5. Accepted by reasoning well or not accepted by reasoning well *(sunijjhāyitaṁ / dunijjhāyitaṁ)*[8].

The same argument is seen in the *Sandaka-sutta* refuting both authority and logic, but in a different way.

1. What is well heard may be true or may be false *(sussutaṁ yathā / sussutaṁ aññathā)*.
2. What is not well heard may be true or may be false *(dussutaṁ yathā / dussutaṁ aññathā)*.
3. What is well reasoned out may be true or may be false *(sutakkitaṁ yathā / sutakkitaṁ aññathā)*.
4. What is not well reasoned out may be true or may be false *(dutakkitaṁ yathā / dutakkitaṁ aññathā)*[9].

As Buddhism does not advocate the theory of an omnipotent creator God, the problem of belief in revelation has no place in Buddhism. Hence it has no place for any authority traditionally accepted by the brahmins and the recluses in contemporary India. Nevertheless, logic seems to have been accepted by Buddhism in a limited sense, not as a means of knowledge for arriving at the truth, but as a tool for presenting a view coherently, sequentially and consistently for better understanding. Defects of logical reasoning also have been shown in the canon. An example of the Fallacy of *Ignorantio Elinchi* is found in

---

[8]   *M.* II, p. 171
[9]   *M.* I, p. 520 ff

the *Mahāsīhanada-sutta* in regard to Sunakkhatta's
accusation against the Buddha. Here the arguer tries to
prove that something is the case but instead he proves
something else. He accused the Buddha saying that the
Buddha preaches the *Dhamma* hammered out by
reasoning, following His own line of inquiry as it
occurred to Him and when He teaches the *dhamma* to
anyone, it leads one to the complete destruction of
suffering when one practises it.

When the Buddha came to know this, the Buddha said:

> "Sunakkhatta is angry and his words are spoken
> with anger. Thinking to discredit the Tathāgata he
> actually praises Him by saying that when He
> teaches the *dhamma* to anyone it leads one to
> the complete destruction of suffering when one
> practises it."

Sunakkhatta was under the impression that psychic
powers are more superior to the destruction of
suffering[10]. The examples of the Fallacy of Begging the
Question, Fallacy of Arguing from Authority, Fallacy of
Composition and the like have been recorded in the
canon to show the incompatibility of the arguments.

As stated in the *Culavyūha-sutta* in the *Suttanipata,*
devising speculation in respect of their views, all the
religious disputants speak of two things due to mistaken
perception - truth and falsehood[11]. Therefore a monk
should cut off inclination to doubt *(takkāsaya)* and
remorse *(kukkucca)*[12]. Hemaka said before the Buddha:

---

[10] *M.* I, p. 68-69
[11] *Sn.* 886
[12] *Sn.* 972

"If any person explained to me previously before hearing Gotama's teaching 'Thus it was. Thus it will be.' all that was hearsay, all that increased my speculation"[13]. Therefore a sage *(muni)* leaving speculation behind is not counted in any category[14]."

📖📖📖

Logic and Authority

X says:	*"The Vedas are revealed texts, therefore they are authoritative."*
Y says:	*"How do you say that?"*
X says:	*"It is said in the Vedas, therefore they are to be taken as authority."*
Y says:	*"But, my friend, how do you prove that?"*
X says:	*"They have been composed by the Vedic seers who had been divinely inspired."*

---

[13] *Sn.* 1089
[14] *takkaṁ pahāya na upeti saṅkhaṁ- Sn.* 209

Evil Kamma is billed and debited

"When doing evil deeds,
the fool is oblivious.
The dullard
is tormented
by his own deeds,
as if burned by fire."

-*Dhammapada*, 36
Translated by Thanissaro Bhikkhu

14. *Criteria of Ethical Judgement in Buddhism*

E thics is a normative science determining norms, ideals and standards for man's behaviour. It examines how man ought to behave and lays principles for that behaviour. While the views of individual philosophers on the subject can be found in different philosophical systems, religious teaching on the subject as expounded by the founders of the religions, commented and supplemented by subsequent commentators, are found in the religions of the world.

Different Views on Ethical Judgement

As an ethical judgement deals with the problem of good and evil, a subjectivist may say that goodness or evilness of an action depends upon one's feelings and intentions.

An objectivist on the other hand may maintain that it corresponds closely to the views of common sense on moral matters. Deontologically the rightness or wrongness of an act depends neither upon the motive from which the act was done nor upon its consequence, but solely upon what kind of act it was; which is often described as duty ethics. Here what is right is considered a duty as opposed to ethical systems advocating the idea of achieving some good state of affairs.

A relativist may hold the view that moral judgement is relative, varying from time to time and society to society, therefore ethics and morality are relative phenomena.

According to utilitarianism an action is right insofar as it tends to produce greatest happiness for the greatest number.

The Buddhist View

According to Buddhism an action may be wholesome (*kusala*), unwholesome *(akusala)* or indeterminate *(avyākata)*. Wholesome and unwholesome actions are ethically significant while indeterminate actions are kammically neutral. The first two kinds in respect of kammic retribution are known as meritorious *(puñña)* and demeritorious *(pāpa)* respectively. Unlike theistic religions, in Buddhism, the moral values of these actions are judged purely on empirical grounds leaving aside any kind of supernatural intervention whatsoever.

Because of the assumption that moral code expresses God's will, the violation of the code is disobedience to the authority of God, hence immorality is disobedience.

Philosophers have argued that this supposition can be accepted only if it can be shown that God is ethically good. Can that be proved? They say it cannot be proved because of the evils found in the world: floods, droughts, cyclones, pestilence, epidemics, cruelty, diseases, premature deaths and so on.

Buddhism is ethical and moral from beginning to the end. Value of moral life is stressed throughout and the retributive effect of an action that manifests itself in this life and the subsequent lives are illustrated without the mediation of any supernatural agent. Free will and responsibility are ascribed to the individual himself making the individual independent in moulding his own 'destiny'. Man being the lord of himself, occupies a unique position in the Buddhist system of ethics. Since Buddhism is specific with regard to moral value of an action, motive and intention of an action are evaluated with reference to righteous or unrighteous means adopted in performing an action. Moreover, the benefit that particular action can vouchsafe to the performer and the others are also taken into consideration together with its outcome as the ultimate good of that particular action.

Primarily, an action can be motivated by either the unwholesome roots of evil: greed *(lobha)*, malice *(dosa)* and delusion *(moha)* or by the wholesome roots of good: non-greed *(alobha)*, non-malice *(adosa)* and non-delusion *(amoha)*. The kammic potentiality lies in the fact of motivation that drives the person to act in that particular manner. Since achieving the end by any means does not justify that particular means according to Buddhism, to classify an action as wholesome, righteous means have to be adopted in performing that action. Assuredly the action must be directed towards one's own good and that of others. For this purpose, several criteria have been prescribed in the Buddhist scriptures. The three principal references *(ādhipateyya)* enunciated in the *Anguttara-nikaya* is significant in this connection.

Three Principal References

1.   Reference   to   one's   own   conscience *(attādhipateyya)*.

It is stated that one must evaluate the action that one is going to perform with reference to one's own conscience. According to some of the modern philosophers, difficulties may crop up when one appeals to conscience, because conscience may be sometimes overwhelmed by prejudice and also one's conscience may be incompatible with the real state of affairs. On grounds of conscience one may justify the killing of an enemy but another may not. One modern ethical philosopher, Bishop Butler, argued that one should therefore refer to one's conscience in deciding what God wishes. The Buddhist standpoint is different. The action is to be judged in terms of the three roots of evil. If one performs an evil action, one's conscience will upbraid him (*attā'pi attānam upavadeyya*). If the conscience is not capable enough to judge the action, one is advised to go to the next criterion.

2.   Reference to conventions in the world (*lokādhipateyya*).

Herein the conventions in the world have to be taken as a criterion for judging an action. According to some of the modern philosophers conventions may differ from society to society and from time to time. For instance, natives of Fiji Islands are morally obliged to bury their aged relatives alive. Pigmies offer their wives to their guests to spend the night with them. Therefore they argue that because of these complications, social conventions cannot be utilized successfully to evaluate an action. In evaluating the moral value of an action, the diversity of conventions does not hinder a Buddhist. In addition to the three roots of evil, one has to ponder over the opinions of the people, specially the way by which the wise would look at the action. If it is evil, one realizes that when the wise come to know it, they would censure him *(anuvicca viññū garaheyyuṁ)*.

3.   Reference to the Doctrine *(dhammādhipateyya)*.

If one fails in evaluating the moral value of an action with reference to the above two criteria, the third criterion, the doctrine, comes to one's aid. "What would be the consequence of this action according to the doctrine that I follow?" Since there is no different interpretations as found in some of the theo-centric religions justifying the slaughtering of those who hold heterodox views, a practising Buddhist is expected to abstain from the evils of harming others. The five precepts, the basic tenets of a Buddhist, are one's criteria. The *dhamma* (doctrine) provides him the direct guideline to evaluate the action. Then one realizes that if one performs an unwholesome action against what the *dhamma* has ordained, the result would be bitter and one will have to be born in a woeful state, a state of downfall, a purgatory *(parammaraṇā apāyaṁ duggatiṁ vinipātaṁ pāṭikankhā)*.[1]

Another criterion is given in the *Veludvāra-sutta* of the *Sanyutta-nikaya*. It focuses the attention on evaluating an action objectively with reference to others' feeling. The discourse in question describes the process of this evaluation at length.

Comparing one's feeling with others' *(attūpanāyika dhammapariyāya)*.

---

[1]   *A.* I, p. 147.

The discourse advises the Aryan disciple to reflect thus: " I am fond of my life, not wanting to die, fond of pleasure and averse to pain. Suppose someone should rob me of my life, it would not be a thing pleasing or delightful to me. If I, in my turn, should rob someone of his life, one fond of his life, not wanting to die, one fond of pleasure and averse to pain, it would not be a thing pleasing or delightful to him. For a state that is not pleasing or delightful to me, how could I inflict upon another?"

As a result of such reflection, he himself abstains from killing living beings and he encourages others to do likewise, and speaks in praise of such abstinence.

Then again the Aryan disciple reflects thus: " If someone should take with thievish intent what I have not given to him, it would not be a thing pleasing or delightful to me. If I, in my turn, should take from another with thievish intent what he has not given me, it would not be a thing pleasing or delightful to him. For a state that is not pleasing or delightful to me, how could I inflict upon another?"

As a result of such reflection, he himself abstains from taking what is not given and he encourages others to do likewise, and speaks in praise of such abstinence.

With reference to other evils also he reflects in the same way. Sexual misconduct, lying, slandering, harsh speech and frivolous talk are mentioned in the discourse in connection with the comparing of one's feeling with that of others. The *sutta* thus employing an objective criterion justifies the fact that one should not do to others what others should not do unto one.[2]

A Universal Criterion of Ethical Judgement

The *Ambalaṭṭhikārāhulovāda-sutta* of the *Majjhima-nikaya* provides us with a moral criterion of universal application. The Buddha addressing the venerable Rahula says that if any action is not beneficial to oneself, not beneficial to others, and not beneficial to both oneself and others, that is an unwholesome action that should be avoided. *(attabyābadhāya parabyābadhāya ubhayabyābadhāya saṁvatteyya .....akusalaṁ)*. On the other hand, if an action is beneficial to oneself, beneficial to others and beneficial to both oneself and others, that is a wholesome action that is to be practised.

The Buddha further advises him to reflect on the pros and cons of an action before it is performed. The criterion given in the discourse is three faceted and applicable to all humans despite the differences of caste, creed, race or colour.[3]

In addition, the Buddhist practices such as Four Divine Abodes *(catu brahmavihāra)*: Loving Kindness, Compassion, Sympathetic Joy and Equanimity and Four Ways of Showing Favour *(catu-sangaha-vatthu)*: Liberality, Kindly Speech, Beneficial Action and

---

[2] *S.* V, p. 3070.
[3] *M.* I, pp. 414-416

Impartiality be can considered as guidelines for ethical actions of moral value.

📖📖📖

One's Actions should be Mirrored before Performance

The Buddha admonishes young Rahula:

> *"What do you think, Rahula, what is the purpose of a mirror?"*

> *"For the purpose of reflection, venerable sir."*

> *"So too, Rahula, an action with the body should be done after repeated reflection; an action by speech should be done after repeated reflection; an action by mind should be done after repeated reflection."*

> *-Ambalaṭṭhikārāhulovāda-sutta, M. I, 416*
> *MLDB, p.524*

Reality is One

"There are not indeed many eternal truths in the world, except by reason of mistaken perception. Devising sophistry in respect of their views, they say that there are two things, truth and falsehood."

-Suttanipata, 886

15. *The Buddhist Analysis of Truth and Reality*

The Pali word for truth is *'sacca'*. In the Buddha's first sermon, *Dhammacakkappavattana-sutta*, a brief account of the four truths named the Four Noble Truths *(cattāri ariyasaccāni)* is given. They are called 'Noble' because they are unique in a religious sense and also they unfold the religious objective of the teaching of the Buddha by analysing the present suffering and unsatisfactory human experience and prescribe a religious mode of behaviour to get out of suffering and dissatisfaction forever. They are called 'Truths' because they are factual statements. The correspondence to facts, coherence and consistency or compatibility with real state of affairs, and verifiability are characteristics of truths.

In the texts, these characteristics are introduced with the words such as 'factual' *(bhūta)*, 'a thing as it really is' *(yathābhūta)*, 'correct' *(taccha)*, 'reliable' *(theta)*, 'trustworthy' *(paccayīka)*, and 'not otherwise' *(anaññathā)*. In a religious sense they are beneficial *(atthasaṁhita)* as they deal with the happiness of all. A person who speaks the truth is 'a person who does not deceive the world' *(avisaṁvādako lokassa)*. As given in the discourse, the Four Noble Truths are:

1. Suffering
2. Cause of Suffering
3. Cessation of Suffering
4. Path leading to the Cessation of Suffering

The factual and noble characteristics of the Four Noble Truths can be seen when they are put into statements or propositions having subject and predicate as follows:

1.   Life is suffering.
2.   Suffering originates from desire.
3.   There is cessation of suffering.
4.   There is the Path leading to the cessation of suffering.

The first proposition brings the present predicament of humans to light since it exhausts the totality of human experience with its description, which is a truth that cannot be denied. The next three truths are based on the fact of the first and analyse the cause, the alleviation of suffering and the measures to be adopted for the alleviation of it. As these four truths together fulfil the religious purpose of Buddha's teaching, they are called Four Noble Truths, the truths par excellence.

The fact that Buddhism has a correct philosophy of life and a correct mode of behaviour based on that philosophy leading to realization is illustrated by the formulation of these Four Noble Truths which were propounded at the very outset of Buddha's career.

Of course there are other truths on the empirical level. Some of them are relevant to the religious mode of behaviour prescribed in Buddhism and some are indeed not. The Buddha was very pertinent in regard to all of those different kinds of truths. Therefore, in the *Abhayarājakumāra-sutta* of the *Majjhima-nikaya*, the Buddha analyses them in respect of their intrinsic characteristics and shows the procedure He adopts in proclaiming them.

The Classification of Propositions According to Truth Value

Herein six kinds of propositions are differentiated, according to which a proposition may be:

1. Untrue, incorrect, not beneficial, and which is also unpleasant and disagreeable to others.

2. True, correct, not beneficial, and which is also unpleasant and disagreeable to others.

3. True, correct, beneficial, and which is also unpleasant and disagreeable to others.

4. Untrue, incorrect, not beneficial, and pleasant and agreeable to others.

5. True, correct, but not beneficial, and pleasant and agreeable to others.

6. True, correct and beneficial and also pleasant and agreeable to others.

The Buddha pronounces only the third and the sixth of these propositions knowing the right time *(kālaññū)*. Further it illustrates the fact that He proclaims only the propositions which are true and beneficial *(atthasaṁhita)* whether they are agreeable or not agreeable, pleasant or unpleasant to them.

The Theory of Correspondence

The theory of correspondence of truth looms large in the *Apaṇṇaka-sutta* of the *Majjhima-nikaya* in connection with the arguments adduced to explain the incontrovertible doctrine *(apaṇṇaka dhamma)*. A practical argument given in the *sutta* proves the significance of the Buddhist proposition of practising good convincingly on experiential considerations:

"Since there actually is another world, one who holds this view 'there is another world' has right view. Since there actually is another world, one who makes the statement 'there is another world' has right speech. Since there actually is another world, one who says 'there is another world' is not opposed to those arahants who know the other world. Since there actually is another world, one who convinces another 'there is another world' convinces him to accept true *dhamma;* because he convinces another to accept true *dhamma*, he does not praise himself and disparage others............ About this a wise man considers thus – if there is another world, then on the dissolution of the body, after death, this good person will reappear in a happy destination, even in the heavenly world. Now whether or not the word of those good recluses and brahmins is true, let me assume that there is no other world. Still this good person is here and now praised by the wise as a virtuous person, one with right view who holds the doctrine of affirmation. And on the other hand, if there is another world, then this good person has made a lucky throw on both counts. Since he is praised by the wise here and now, and since on the dissolution of the body, after death, he will reappear in a happy destination, even in the heavenly world. He has rightly accepted and undertaken this incontrovertible teaching in such a way that it extends to both sides and excludes the unwholesome alternative".[1]

The Theory of Coherence and Consistency

Coherence and consistency are also considered as essential factors for judging the validity of an assertion. It has been shown that specially in discussions and arguments one should maintain coherence and consistency throughout in order to maintain the validity and reliability of his assertion. Thus in the *Cūlasaccaka-sutta* of the *Majjhima-nikaya* the Buddha keeps on reminding Saccaka the defects of his contribution in the discussion:

> "Pay attention Saccaka, pay attention to how you reply! What you said before does not agree with what you said afterwards, nor does what you said afterwards agree with what you said before".[2]

The Theory of Verification

Verifiability is also another characteristic of the doctrine. Logical Positivists held the view that since the meaning of a statement is its verifiability, a statement devoid of

---

[1]   *M.* I, 403-4
[2]   *M.* I, 232

verification of its cognitive meaning of truth or falsity is meaningless.

The truths expounded in the form of doctrine in Buddhism are verifiable by perception and extrasensory perception and it is stated in the *Anguttara-nikaya* that the doctrine and discipline shine when laid bare and not when covered. It is free from metaphysical or theological or divine secrets of any kind. Unlike Upanishads it was not taught to a selected few, but meant for all and open to all. For the good it is uncovered like the light *(satam ca vivaṭo hoti āloko passataṁ iva)³.*

In the often quoted formula where the characteristics of the dhamma are given, it is mentioned that the dhamma has the qualities of: 'yielding results here and now' *(sandiṭṭhiko),* 'immediate results' *(akālika),* 'inviting others to come and see' *(ehi passika),* and 'should be realized by the wise each for himself'.

Evidently, these epithetic clauses are meaningful only in the context of verifiability of the *dhamma.* In a discourse addressed to elder Upavāna, it is stated that the consciousness of the sensation of the sensual objects and the passion therein make one convinced of the above verifiable qualities of the *dhamma⁴.* The Buddha is praised as an eyewitness of *dhamma* that dispels the dangers *(sakkhi dhammaṁ parissaya vinayaṁ)⁵.*

---

³ *Sn.* 763
⁴ *S.* IV. p. 40
⁵ *Sn.* 921

The Theory of Double Truth

Later in the *Abhidhamma,* there is the conception of double truth developed for the sake of differentiating abstruse technical exposition of the *dhamma.* This distinction seems to have developed on the earlier division of propositions having 'direct' or 'drawn out' meaning *(nitattha)* and 'indirect' or 'to be drawn out' meaning *(neyyattha).* The former is an explicit statement with definite meaning such as a statement dealing with impermanence, suffering and non-substantiality, which is to be taken as it is. The latter is a statement of common understanding based on the conventions in the world such as 'one individual, two individuals' etc. In fact, in the ultimate sense individual is nothing but a conglomeration of five aggregates.

It is stressed that if one were to overlook the different significance of these statements and interpret the former to mean that there is something here in this world which is permanent, happy and substantial, and the latter, going beyond the conventions in the world, to mean a permanent entity as individual can be found in the world, one would be totally wrong since they are misrepresentations of the Buddha.[6]

Later with the development of *abhidhamma,* in order to facilitate the technicalities involved in its exposition, two truths were evolved on the distinction outlined in the 'direct' and 'indirect' division of the *dhamma.* These two forms of truth are called Conventional Truth *(Sammuti sacca)* and Ultimate Truth *(paramattha sacca).*

---

[6] *A.* II, p. 60

The first refers to the general turn of speech, the common use of the language, which is discursive and marked with parables, similes and anecdotes. The second is impersonal, technical and abstract, and describes the ultimate categories called dhammas: Consciousness, Mental Concomitants, Matter and *Nibbāna* and the inter-relationship of the first three categories in minute detail.

It is stated that both kinds of truth are true and valid corresponding to the sphere they deal with. For it is said in the *Anguttara-nikāyaṭṭhakathā*:

> "Common language is true as it is convention-based, and so are the words of ultimate truth also true as they reveal the real nature of dhammas."

> *(saṁketavacanaṁ saccaṁ*
> *lokasammutikāraṇaṁ*
> *paramatthavacanaṁ saccaṁ*
> *dhammānaṁ tathalakkhaṇaṁ)*[7]

Reality and Truth

Nibbāna is the reality propounded in Buddhism. It is the unique ultimate truth described in Buddhism. Nevertheless, in the early Pali canonical texts, reality is also introduced by the word *'sacca'*, the truth.

The *Suttanipāta* says:

> "There is only one truth; there is no second, about which men might dispute. They speak of

---

[7] *AA.* II. p. 118

different truths, therefore the recluses do not proclaim the one truth."[8]

However, the stanza in question is interpretative. Reality is the Supreme Bliss, *Nibbāna*.

📖📖📖

How the Truth-seeker should be

Nan-in, a Japanese master during the Meiji era (1868-1912) received a university professor who came to inquire about Zen. Nan-in served tea. He poured his visitor's cup full, and then kept on pouring. The Professor watched the tea overflow until he no longer could restrain himself.

"It is over full. No more will go in!"

"Like this cup," Nan-in said, "you are full of your opinions and speculation, how can I show you Zen unless you first empty your cup?"

-Surekha V. Limaye
Zen (Buddhism) and Mysticism, p. 51

---

[8] *Sn.* 884

Empiricism with a Difference

"The emphasis that 'knowing' (jānaṁ) must be based on 'seeing' (passaṁ) or direct perceptive experience, makes Buddhism a form of empiricism. We have, however, to modify the use of the term somewhat to mean not only that all our knowledge is derived from sense-experience but from extrasensory experience as well."

-K. N. Jayatilleke
Early Buddhist Theory of Knowledge, pp, 463-4

16. *Empiricism and Buddhism*

A s Buddhism is empiricist in its approach to human problems and their resolution, it is considered a unique feature particular to Buddha's teaching. Many scholars, both Eastern and Western, have expressed their concern and personal views with reference to this characteristic special to Buddhism among other world religions.

Empiricism in Western Philosophy

In modern Western philosophy, empiricism ascribes a predominant place to sense experience. Doubts about the rationalistic theory of knowledge is said to have led to the search for a theory amicable to common human behaviour that we experience in our day to day life. When England was experiencing rapid development in industrial and commercial activities, the rationalistic approaches of philosophers such as Plato and Descartes, who held that true knowledge is already within us in the form of innate ideas with which we are born and not acquired through our senses, were challenged by a new generation of philosophers. Hence in the 17th century they began to formulate a system of philosophy taking sense experience as the source and basis of what we know. Since the theory in question is consistent with human experience and attempts to understand knowledge in terms of sense experience, it is called empiricism.

Francis Bacon (1561- 1626) and John Locke (1632-1704) after him, not being professional philosophers, but being practical men of affairs, who had no interest in abstract philosophical problems discussed by different philosophers over the centuries, argued on the basis of sense experience and introduced the new empiricist way of thinking to Western philosophy. They emphasised the fact that there is no knowledge other than the experiential. Therefore empiricism is considered as a theory of knowledge which gives predominance to experience and what is empirically observed. The later philosophers have contributed their own interpretations to the empiricist thought thus making the system a fully developed one.

The Empiricist Tendency in Buddhism

The Buddha asserted that anyone who follows the path prescribed by Him can realise truth by himself without the help of any external agency whatsoever. Therefore the inherent characteristics of the teaching of the Buddha delineated in the formula quoted often, five important terms have been used amounting to the empiricist approach pertaining to the fundamental nature of the doctrine:

a. It is advantageous and visible in this very life (*sandiṭṭhika*).
b. It yields immediate results and is timeless (*akālika*).
c. As it is open to all and free from any secrecy it can be examined (*ehipassika*).
d. It can be entered upon and it leads to the goal of Nibbana (*opanaika*).
e. It is to be realised by the wise individually (*paccattaṁ veditabbo viññūhi*).

Evidently, the pre-eminent place given to observation, examination and experimentation in Buddhism has drawn the attention of philosophers and scholars on religion. Radhakrishnan referring to the Buddha and Buddhism remarked in his 'Indian Philosophy':

> "His method is that of psychological analysis. He endeavoured to rid Himself of all illegitimate speculation, build from the raw material of experience, and assist the spiritual growth of suffering humanity by an honest and unbiased expression of the results of His thought and experience. According to Him, if a man sees things as they really are, he will cease to pursue shadows and cleave to the great reality of goodness."

And further stressing the pride of place accorded to experience in Buddhism, he says:

> "Laying aside metaphysical speculations, He traces out the reign of law and order in the world of experience. Understanding, according to Him, is to be limited to the field of experience, the laws which it can explore."[1]

The empiricist approach is the 'scientific attitude' in the language of modern science based on empirical investigation. A. K. Warder who wrote 'Indian Buddhism' is convinced of the empiricist approach found in the discourses and says that the general method of discussion is that of an empirical and rational inquiry basing

---

[1]   *IP.* I. p. 360

emphasis on the empirical aspect.[2] Warder therefore states:

> "The doctrine is not speculative but empiricist. The Buddha emphatically rejected all speculative opinions (drsti) and propounded no such opinion Himself, only an empiricist account of conditioned origination and the way to end unhappiness."[3]

Buddhism advocates both sense perception and extrasensory perception as valid means of knowledge. Extrasensory perception is a result of the meditative absorption recommended in the Buddhist path to realisation. Therefore K. N. Jayatilleke explaining the characteristics of the theory of dependent origination particular to Buddhism maintains that it is based on inductive inferences and that those inferences are made on the data of perception, normal and paranormal. He further states that what is considered to constitute knowledge are direct inferences made on the basis of such perceptions and all the knowledge that the Buddha and His disciples claim to have in 'knowing and seeing', except for the knowledge of Nirvana, appears to be of this nature.[4]

> "The Buddhist theory is therefore empirical since it spoke only of observable causes without any metaphysical pre-suppositions of any substrata behind them. It closely resembles the Regularity theory except for the fact that it speaks of the empirical necessity *(avitathatā, v. supra, 768)* of

---

[2] *IB.* p. 299.

[3] *IB.* p. 377

[4] *EBTK.* p. 457

the causal sequence or concomitance and does not seem to hold that all inductive inferences are merely probable *(v. supra, 758)."*[5]

Buddhism is not based on any kind of metaphysical theory or on an authority founded on revelation or on an indirect proof related to *a priori* reasoning in the sense of logic. According to Buddhism, all these are unsatisfactory as means of knowledge. But it is preached as a verifiable hypothesis, which can be investigated and empirically realised individually by the wise. All the events from the time of witnessing the four signs, which prompted prince Siddhattha to renounce the household life, until he attained the supreme Enlightenment are grounded on personal experience. He realised that birth, disease, decay, death, frustration, disappointment and despair that every individual has to experience in his daily life amount to suffering. As the peace of mind was disturbed by the tragic situation that humankind has to experience, prince Siddhattha was tempted to look for a panacea. The figure of the recluse that he encountered as the fourth sign prompted him to renounce the world in search of truth, and he spent the subsequent six years with several teachers investigating and experimenting the ways and means of arriving at the truth. In the texts two of these teachers are specially mentioned, Alara Kalama and Uddaka Ramaputta, under whom he managed to attain up to the third immaterial absorption called the Base of Nothingness and the fourth immaterial absorption known as the Base of Neither Perception Nor Non-Perception respectively. As he was not satisfied with the meditative experience that he could achieve under these teachers he began to practise a course of action followed by self-mortifying ascetics of his day. In the

---

[5]   *EBTK*. p. 453

Ariyapariyesana-sutta, the *Mahāsaccaka-sutta* and the
Mahāsīhanāda-sutta of the *Majjhima-nikaya* the
personal experience He gained by practising these
austere asceticism and the ways of practising them are
recorded with some details.

As stated in the *Mahāsīhanāda-sutta,* in order to arrive at
a state free from grief *(asoka),* free from death *(amata)*
and free from defilement *(asaṁkiliṭṭha)* he began to
practise penance of self-mortification prevalent among
the ascetics, Ājivikas and Jains. Among these different
types of asceticism, he followed the practices called
'tapassi' amounting to austere asceticism, *'lūkha'* that
gives up association with humans and *'pavivitta'*
advocating complete isolation. For six years as a seeker
after truth, with the thought that even a small living thing
may not be crushed with the feet, he developed
compassion and non-violence extending even towards a
drop of water.[6] In his four bodily postures of sitting,
walking, standing and lying down he was attentive and
compassionate. He performed sacrifice with the hope of
achieving purity through sacrifice *(yaññena suddhi)* and
with the aim of acquiring purity from food he observed
fasting, but these experiences did not yield any
substantial result whatsoever. Even before his training
under the teachers he was represented as practising
several types of yoga practices which were in vogue
among the ascetic groups in India at the time, but
without any successful result. These practises are listed
in the *Mahāsaccaka-sutta* of the *Majjhima-nikaya.*

When the Buddha was recollecting his practice of
asceticism under Alara Kalama as well as Uddaka
Ramaputta, it is stated that since they lived 'knowing'

---

[6]   *M.* I. p. 78

(*jānaṁ*) and 'seeing' (*passaṁ*) the states that they professed, He also put forth His energy to experience those states of absorption. That shows the fact that those states were not merely theoretical but experiential and to be achieved by practice. The discourse further records the austere ascetic practices He engaged in even after going away from the teachers. The ascetic Gotama clenched his teeth with his tongue pressed against his palate in order to subdue, dominate and restrain the mind. Then perspiration dripped from his armpits. Then he practised non-breathing meditation and stopped breathing in and out through the mouth or nose resulting in the loud noise of wind escaping through his auditory passages. When he continued the pràctice he felt as if a strong man were to cleave his head with a sharp-edged sword. As if a strong man were to clamp a turban on his head with a tight leather strap and a skilled cattle-butcher or his apprentice were to cut through the stomach with a sharp butcher's knife. There appeared a bad headache and a fierce heat all over his body just as setting fire to a weaker man having taken hold of him by two strong men. His experience on non-breathing meditation and other austere ascetic practices have been vividly described in the discourses. It was on examination and experimentation that the Buddha proclaimed the futility of those ascetic practices.

The Buddhist teaching of suffering, three characteristics of existence and dependent origination are empirically based. It is vindicated by the relevant discourses where these doctrinal themes are discussed. Therefore it is quite clear that Buddhism is neither a kind of metaphysical speculation nor a revelation, but a teaching based on empirical facts and that it is to be experienced.

📖📖📖

Rationalism in a Different Context

"Although there is little evidence that any of the basic doctrines of Buddhism are derived by reason, we sometimes meet with the Buddha recommending his doctrines on rational grounds. This is particularly evident where his sermons are addressed to the viññū or the elite, who seem to represent open minded rationalist."

-K. N. Jayatilleke
Early Buddhist Theory of Knowledge, p. 405

17. Is Buddhism Rationalistic?

T he scholars who wrote on the Buddha and Buddhism have often referred to the Buddha as a rationalist and Buddhism as rationalistic. They have come to this conclusion on different grounds. To begin with, let us see what Radhakrishnan has to say in this regard. Certainly, he begins by saying that "we cannot consider Buddha a rationalist" and continues:

> "Rationalism is defined as 'the mental habit of using reason for the destruction of religious beliefs'. Buddha did not set out with the intention of reaching negative results. Being a disinterested seeker after truth, He did not start with any prejudice. Yet He is a rationalist, since He wished to study reality or experience without any reference to supernatural revelation. In this matter Buddha is at one with modern scientists, who are of opinion that the idea of supernatural interference should not be introduced into the logical interpretation of natural phenomena. Buddha had so firm a grip of the connectedness of things that He would not tolerate miraculous interference of the cosmic order or magical disturbances of material life."[1]

While describing Buddhism and the particular nature of the Buddha's rationalistic approach, he says further that the Buddha relied on reason and experience and that He wished to lead men by mere force of logic to His view to establish a "religion within the bounds of pure reason".

---

[1]   *IPh.* I, p. 359

He seems to have maintained that Buddhism is rationalistic because it rejects supernatural revelation of any sort and also because of the pre-eminent place given to logic and pure reasoning in it. Truly, the first part of his assertion is in agreement with what we know from the canon, but the second part that the Buddha tried to establish a religion on the force of logic in the bounds of pure reason, is to be taken with a pinch of salt. Because, Sunakkhatta's observation that the Buddha had no distinctive knowledge and vision more than that of other men and that He preached a doctrine which was a product of reasoning and speculation and self-evident, was totally denied by the Buddha.[2] According to the Buddha's view, logical reasoning may be true or false, just as that which is said to be revealed and handed down orally from generation to generation.

To some of the scholars, who wrote on Buddhism, the Buddha was an out and out rationalist because of the fact that He rejected dogmatism. Truly Buddhism is opposed to dogmatism of every kind. Bhattacharya in his *"Basic Conception of Buddhism"* quotes the famous *Kālāma-sutta* in support of his view that the Buddha was not a dogmatist but a rationalist.[3] Although the *sutta* in question, while rejecting logical reasoning as a valid means of knowledge, recommends free inquiry, he seems to have taken rationalism in a general sense to mean freedom of thought.

To name Buddhism as rationalistic Poussin has taken a different stance in his *"Way to Nirvana"*. According to him, Buddhism is rationalistic since the Buddha was non-mystical and succeeded in explaining the cosmos and

---

[2]   *M.* I, p. 68
[3]   Bhattācharya V. – *The Basic Conception of Buddhism*, p. 9ff.

human destiny without recourse to any kind of metaphysical agent. This scholar seems to have conjectured that Buddhism is rationalistic because there is no place for supernaturalism and mysticism in it.

Rationalism in Western Philosophy

Although these scholars have viewed Buddhism as rationalistic on different grounds, it is very difficult to pass judgement on its rationalistic outlook without taking the use of the term in modern philosophy into consideration. Also, since these scholars are not consistent in their use of the term, it is necessary to find out its philosophical connotation in modern Western philosophy. According to which, paradigm of knowledge is the non-sensory intellectual intuition that God would have into the working of all things. In other words, the criterion of truth is not sensory but intellectual, deductive and related to mathematics. The continental philosophers such as Plato, Descartes, Leibniz and Spinoza are usually named as rationalists. They asserted that by employing certain procedures of reason alone one could arrive at knowledge, which would not change under any circumstance. They further maintained that such knowledge could not be found through sense experience but have to seek for it only in the realm of the mind.

Rationalism Versus Empiricism

Often in discussions on Western philosophy, the theory of rationalism is contrasted with empiricism, which has given pride of place to sense experience. And also it is a historical fact that empiricism evolved in the west against rationalism, which had taken hold as a system of philosophy. In this connection it is plausible for us to see whether the Buddha in any sense considered certain premises as being self-evidently true and based His teaching on those premises to name Him as a rationalist. The Buddha did not attempt to evolve a system of deductive metaphysics based on axioms or premises, which are self-evident and true as products of reasoning. Buddhism is empiricist since it is inductive and devoid of *a priori* reasoning.   Since Buddhism advocates an empirical approach in seeking knowledge, it is not rationalistic in the philosophical sense of the term.

Nevertheless, as these scholars have done, taking the role that plays by reason in search of truth, the term rationalism can be used more broadly for any anti-clerical and anti-authoritarian system, because Buddhism addresses to one's reason. In general usage 'reason' is intellect or intellectual acumen and the due exercise of the faculty of thought. Therefore in that general sense, Buddhism is rationalistic and its approach is rational. Not being dogmatic, it addresses to one's reason for critical examination of facts. It is to be realized by thoughtful reflection with the exercise of reflective reasoning.

The Buddhist theory of knowledge begins with receiving information from the external world and subjecting that into thoughtful reflection (*yoniso manasikāra*). Literally it means 'reflecting by way of origin'. This leads one to right understanding while unthoughtful reflection leads one to wrong understanding. Thoughtful reflection tends to modify one's behaviour and attitudes together with one's lifestyle. Therefore several steps of this intellectual exercise have been described in the discourses including the *Kīṭāgiri-sutta* of the *Majjhima-nikaya*. It is a rational evaluation of sense data leading one to destroy one's ignorance and achieve wisdom. Since Buddhism considers ignorance as one of the fundamental factors for man's suffering, the path envisaged in Buddhism leads to understanding and wisdom. One who thoughtfully reflects upon the sense data including what he has heard becomes convinced and develops confidence to know the *Dhamma* and proceeds on as following:

I. Because of confidence he draws close.
II. Drawing close he sits down nearby.
III. Sitting down nearby he lends his ear.
IV. Lending his ear he listens to the doctrine.
V. Having heard the doctrine he remembers it.
VI. He then tests the meaning of things he has born in mind.
VII. While testing the meaning they are approved of.
VIII. There being approval of the things, desire is born.
IX. With desire born he makes an effort.
X. Having made an effort he weighs it up.
XI. Having weighed it up he strives.
XII. Finally being self-resolute he realises with his person the Highest Truth.

Now, in this connection the Buddha has pointed out four expositions pertaining to a disciple who has followed the instruction faithfully and lives according to it. He begins to realise:

I. "The Teacher is the Lord; a disciple am I; the Lord knows, I do not know."
II. He comprehends that the Teacher's instruction is a furthering in growth and a giving of strength.
III. He puts his shoulder to the wheel and thinks:

"Gladly would I be reduced to skin and sinews and bones and let my body's flesh and blood dry up if there comes to be a vortex of energy so that which is not yet won might be won by human strength, by human energy, by human striving."

IV.   One of the two fruits is to be expected by the disciple who adheres to the Teacher's instruction and lives in unison with it. Profound knowledge here and now, and if there is any basis for rebirth remaining, the state of non-return.

It is to be noted that one is advised to repose one's confidence in the Buddha or in the doctrine only after thoughtful reflection. Buddhism encourages one to exercise one's reflective reasoning ability for free inquiry, freedom of expression, autonomy of moral judgement, right to dissent, free will and for personal responsibility. As there is no external agency to atone the evil effects of one's actions, one has to be responsible for one's own actions.

In the *Vimaṁsaka-sutta* of the *Majjhima-nikaya*, the Buddha, addressing the monks, outlines this method of reasoning thus:

"A monk, O monks, who is an inquirer, not knowing how to guage another's mind, should investigate the Tathagata with respect to two kinds of states, states cognizable through the eye and through the ear thus: 'Are there found in the Tathagata or not any defiled states cognizable through the eye or through the ear?' When he investigates Him, he comes to know: 'No defiled

states cognizable through the eye or through the
ear are found in the Tathagata.'"

The discourse continuing this method of rational
investigation further, winds up with the following
conclusion as its outcome:

> "O monks, when anyone's faith has been planted,
> rooted and established in the Tathagata through
> these reasons, terms and phrases, his faith is said
> to be supported by reason, rooted in vision
> (*ākāravatīsaddhā dassana mūlikā*), firm, it is
> invincible by any recluse or brahmin or god or
> Mara or Brahma or by anyone in the world. That
> is how, monks, there is an investigation of the
> Tathagata in accordance with the *Dhamma*, and
> that is how the Tathagata is well investigated in
> accordance with the *Dhamma*."[4]

Therefore, since pre-eminent place is given to rational
understanding and evaluation of data with thoughtful
reflection, rationalism found in Buddhism is distinctly
different either from rationalism in Western philosophy or
from logical reasoning prevalent among ancient Indian
materialists.

$$\text{□□□}$$

---

[4]   *M.* I, p. 318ff.

How could there be Vicarious Salvation?

"These greedy liars propagate deceit,
And fools believe the fictions they repeat:
He who has eyes can see the sickening sight:
Why does not Brahma set his creatures right?
If his wide power no limits can restrain,
Why is his hand so rarely spread to bless?
Why are his creatures all condemned to pain?
Why does he not to all give happiness?
Why do fraud, lies, and ignorance prevail?
Why triumphs falsehood,-truth and justice fail?"

-Bhūridatta Jataka
J. Vol, No. 543
Tr. Cowell

18. *Man and Society in Buddhist Perspective*

A ccording to Buddhism, among all the terrestrial and celestial beings, man occupies the most desirable position. Herein, by the word 'man' the entire humankind should be understood. It is stated that to be born as a human is a rare event even as the birth of a Buddha, the availability of the good Dhamma and one's opportunity to listen to it. This point is illustrated in the *Bālapaṇḍita-sutta* of the *Majjhima-nikaya* with the simile of the blind turtle and the yoke. The Buddha addressing the monks says:

> "Suppose a man throws into the sea a yoke with one hole in it, and the east wind carries it to the west, and the west wind carried it the east, and the north wind carries it to the south, and the south wind carried it to the north. Suppose there were a blind turtle that came up once at the end of each century. What do you think, O monks? Would that blind turtle put its neck into that yoke with one hole in it?"

When the monks reply:

> "It might, Sir, sometime or other at the end of a long period."

The Buddha continues:

> "O monks, the blind turtle would take less time to put its neck into that yoke with a single hole in it than a fool, once gone to perdition, would take to

> regain the human state, I say. Why is that?
> Because there is no practising of the Dhamma
> there, no practising of what is righteous, no doing
> of what is wholesome, no performance of merit.
> There mutual devouring prevails, and the
> slaughter of the weak." (*M*. III, p. 169).

The fact that to be born as a human being is a rare event
is emphasised in Buddhism, seemingly for two reasons.
Firstly, to bring out the enormous suffering that a person
has to undergo in his wandering in the cyclic existence
of birth and death. Secondly, in order to inculcate an
awareness of urgency in the mind of the people to
practise Dhamma, be righteous and to perform
wholesome actions leading to realisation. Simply, one
should be good and do good during his lifetime making
the best out of living a human life in order to get rid of
suffering and realise the supreme Bliss.

Who is Man?

The Pali words for man are '*manussa*' and '*māṇava*',
which according to popular etymology are defined to
mean "offspring of *manu*", the first mythical man on
earth, who according to Hindu myths, the earliest man to
be born. This definition, however, is found in Pali
commentaries and Pali grammatical works. (e. g.
"*manuno apaccā'ti manussā, porāṇā pana bhaṇanti*"[1].
"*manuno apaccā puttā māṇavā*" – *Rupasiddhi*). Side by
side with these definitions, there is an attempt among the
Pali scholiasts to give an ethical twist to the word in
conformity with the Buddhist ethics by deriving the word

---

[1]   *KhpA*. p. 123

from '*mana*', the mind, which originated from √man - to think. Hence, we find in the *Vimāna-vatthu* commentary as well as in the *Suttanipāta* commentary the definition "*manassa ussannatāya manussā*", "because of the fullness of the mind they are called men". They, however, ascribe the definition to Poranas, the ancients and say further that they are the people inhabiting Jambudipa, Aparagoyāna, Uttarakuru and Pubbavideha, thus exhausting the entire planet earth according to ancient Indian geography.[2] Evidently, the word is Indo-European in origin and connected with the Gothic '*manna*' and English 'man' and traceable back to Vedic '*manusya*'. However, the latter Pali definition coincides in meaning with the word '*Homo Sapiens*' the name given to modern man by anthropologists. Another popular word used to denote man in Pali is '*nara*', which might have originated among the early Indo-European people to denote masculinity of man. (Compare with Latin '*neriosus*' meaning 'mascular').

Because of the behavioural pattern of man, three kinds of man are distinguished from man proper on ethical considerations: man doomed to purgatory (*manussa-nerayika*), man living as spirits (*manussa-peta*) and man living as animals (*manussa-tiracchāna*).[3]

A Unique Position is Ascribed to Man in Buddhism

Man occupies a unique position among all the living things, for he has the ability to work out his own

---

[2] *Vimanavatthu Aṭṭhakathā, p. 18*
[3] *Ibid,* p. 23

salvation. He is considered the highest in the hierarchy of beings because of the power that he can wield for the welfare of himself and others. He is not considered as a penitent sinner who should pray for vicarious help for his own salvation. It is emphasised that the coveted position human beings occupy among all the beings cannot be challenged by any god or Mara or Brahma, the creator-god of Hinduism. Man is given full autonomy of judgement with regard to alternative ethical conduct thereby enabling him to model his own destiny. Only a man can become a Buddha or Bodhisatta. The realisation of the Buddhist ideal cannot be accomplished by a being born as a god of the fine material sphere, much less, of beings who have been born in the spirit world, ghost world, purgatory and animal kingdom. Man has the power of developing his brains to its full capacity together with penetrative wisdom (*paṭisambhidā*) to attain the highest goal in Buddhism. The Buddhist concept of man is a deviation from the theistic concept of man in any world religion. Man has evolved to be what he is, over a long period of billions of years, the scientists would say. Buddhism does not go to the extent of speaking on the origin of man or the other species and satisfy the daft curiosity of people by concocting stories of creation, but man has been given the pride of place and responsibility for his own salvation. Hamlet in the Shakespearean play exclaimed:

"What a piece of work is man? How noble in reason! How infinite in faculty! In form, and moving, how express and admirable! In action, how like an angel! In apprehension, how like a god! The beauty of the world! The paragon of animals! And yet...... what is this quintessence of dust?"

Man has all the excellence, grace and dignity as Shakespeare expressed his wonder through Hamlet. But it is a pity that "few are there amongst men who go beyond the cycle of birth and death. The rest of mankind is only run about on the bank."[4]

Man and Society

Man is born into society, brought up in society and he continues to live in society until his death. An ascetic, too, leaves behind all his encumbrances of household life and departs to forest, carries with him the experience he acquired when he was living in society. Man being a social animal, he acquires his human nature or humane qualities from living in society and maintains relations through communication with the other members who constitute society. No man on earth can develop his personality without the help of any kind of human society. The impact society makes on an individual is so strong that it should be considered as the most fundamental and important factor which builds the character of an individual. A child from his birth is under social influence, because he learns from others, firstly from parents and then from teachers and others. Unlike among other species, human child needs mother's care and protection for several years. He lives with others. When he is grown up to be a man, he develops communication with others weaving a network of relationship with others. He is caught up in the web of obligations and commitments to his fellow beings called society. There is no society without humans and no humans without society. This interdependence of society

---

[4] *Dhp.* 85

and man is persisting not only for the sake of mutual survival but also for the fulfilment of higher ideals related to both man and society. Society existed long before we are born into it and it will continue to exist even long after we are dead and gone.

In the interaction between man and society, society dominates man channelling him on the proper path, instructing him on values, rights, duties, manners and behavioural patterns and many more and directs him to live a meaningful and purposeful life. On the other hand, man also contributes his share to society as an active member of it by way of continuing his social heritage or reshaping it ideologically.

Buddhism, Man and Society

The inter-relationship of man and society is accepted in Buddhism. Hence social ethics in Buddhism is for the welfare of both man and society. The Five Precepts (*pañcasīla*), the Four Sublime Abodes (*cattāro brahmavihārā*), the Four Ways of Showing Favour (*Cattāri saṁgaha vatthūni*) and the Ten Wholesome Deeds (dasakusala) often discussed in the canonical texts vindicate Buddhism's social concern taking the individual as an integral part of it. Therefore Buddhist ethics become meaningful only in the context of society.

Sublime Abodes are: Loving Kindness, Compassion, Altruistic or Sympathetic Joy and Equanimity. Needless to say these mental attitudes are to be developed in relation to others in society. In the same way the Four Ways of Showing Favour, namely by liberality, kindly speech, beneficial actions and impartiality are to be practised for the sake of others. The Five Precepts, too, ensure one's social position as a constituent part of society. With reference to Ten Wholesome Deeds, the first four precepts are discussed in the *Sāleyyaka-sutta* of the *Majjhima-nikaya* in detail.[5] The Ten Wholesome Deeds are discussed in relation to one's conduct of body, word and mind.

Herein the Buddha says:

> "And how, householders, are the three kinds of bodily conduct not in accordance with the Dhamma, unrighteous conduct? Here someone kills living beings; he is murderous, bloody-handed, given to blows and violence, merciless to living beings. He takes what is not given; he takes by way of theft the wealth and property of others in the village or forest. He misconducts himself in sensual pleasures; he has intercourse with women who are protected by their mother and father, brother, sister, or relatives, who have a husband, who are protected by law, and even with those who are garlanded in token of betrothal. That is how there are three kinds of bodily conduct not in accordance with the Dhamma, unrighteous conduct."

> "And how, householders, are there four kinds of verbal conduct not in accordance with the Dhamma, unrighteous conduct? Here someone speaks falsehood. When summoned to a court, or to a meeting, or to his relatives' presence, and questioned as a witness thus: 'So good man, tell what you know.' Not knowing, he says, 'I know', or knowing, he says, 'I do not know', not seeing,

---

[5]   *M.* I, p. 286

he says 'I see', or seeing, he says, 'I do not see';
in full awareness he speaks falsehood for his own
ends, or for another's ends, or for some trifling
worldly end."

In this way the discourse describes the rest of the
wrongful verbal behaviour related to carrying tales, harsh
speech and gossiping and then the mental attitudes of
coveting, ill will and wrong view together with the
positive aspects of all the ten. It is quite clear that these
ethical standards laid down in Buddhism are expressive
and relevant only in the framework of social living.

The Dignity of Man

"Your own self is
your own mainstay,
for who else could your mainstay be?
With you yourself well-trained
you obtain the mainstay
hard to obtain."

-Dhammapada, 160
Translated by Thanissaro Bhikkhu

Only What is Pragmatic

Once the Exalted One while staying at Kosambi in Siæsapâ
Grove gathered up a few Siæsapâ leaves in his hand and
said to the monks:

> "What would you think, monks, which are the
> more numerous, just this mere handful of Siæsapâ
> leaves I have here in my hand, or those in the grove
> overhead?"

> "Very few in number, Lord, are the leaves in the
> handful gathered up by the Exalted one; much are
> in number those overhead."

> "Just so, monks, much more in number are those
> things that I have found out, but not revealed; very
> few are the things I have revealed. And why,
> monks, I have not revealed them? Because they are
> not concerned with profit, they are not rudiments
> of the holy life, they conduce not to revulsion, to
> dispassion, to cessation, to tranquillity, to full
> comprehension, to the perfect wisdom, to Nibbāna.
> That is why I have not revealed them."

- S. V, 370

19. *Pragmatic and Utilitarian Approach in Buddhism*

Buddhism is recognised as a pragmatic religion based on a pragmatic philosophy. Undoubtedly, the emphasis that Buddhism lays on practice prompted the scholars who wrote on Buddhism to introduce Buddhism as a pragmatic religion and philosophy. Buddhism, even in its earlier form, being a religion maintaining a worldview of its own, recommends a proper moral conduct for practice and realisation of the goal it advocates. Since it proclaims a scheme of conduct to be practised for the betterment of one's life here and hereafter, and for the attainment of the supreme Bliss, it can be aptly named as a religion of practice. Assuredly, Buddhism is pragmatic as it is to be practised deliberately. It is also utilitarian as it is concerned only about what is useful for the attainment of the goal it enunciates.

Scholars on Buddhist Approach

Mrs. Rhys Davids has used both epithets with reference to the Buddha and Buddhism. According to her, the Buddha can be called a utilitarian in the sense of being a pragmatist for whom truth is what 'works'. She further remarks in elucidation of her view:

> "Utilitarian might be urged with some weight. 'Rationalistic' surely not. In the very *sutta* chosen to illustrate the latter, the *Kālāma* discourse, rational grounds for testing the gospel are only cited to be put aside....... The test to be used is

'What effect will this teaching produce on my life?' "[1]

Poussin used the word 'pragmatique' while referring to Buddhism.[2] Hiriyanna, in his 'Outlines of Indian Philosophy', naming Buddhism as pragmatic says further:

> "It is pragmatic. The Buddha taught only what is necessary for overcoming evil whose prevalence is, according to Him, the chief characteristic of life".

Continuing his argument, he quotes the parable known as the Handful of *Siṁsapā* Leaves, to highlight the principle that guided the Buddha in His numerous discourses. The Buddha picking up a handful of *siṁsapā* leaves dwelt on the fact that what he had comprehended was much more, like the *siṁsapā* leaves in the forest, and the little that He had revealed was comparable to the handful of leaves in His hand. According to him, the Buddha was a pragmatist, because He neither found time, nor He had a need to unravel metaphysical subtleties. He was thus practical in His teaching.[3]

K. N. Jayatilleke strongly holds that the Buddha was a pragmatist. He adduces many an instance from the canon together with the Parable of the Arrow, the Parable of the Raft and the Questions to be Set Aside (*avyākata*) in support of his view.[4] To Conze, however, Buddhist pragmatism is of a different kind, which he introduced as

[1] Quoted in *EBTK.* pp. 356-7
[2] *Op. Cit.*
[3] *OIPh.* p. 137
[4] *EBTK.* p. 337 ff

'dialectical', 'pragmatic' and 'psychological'. Concluding his observation he says:

> "We can therefore, say with some truth that Buddhist thinking tends in the direction what we called pragmatism."[6].

Although Buddhism advocates a pragmatic and utilitarian religious practice of its own, free from prayer and worship as well as rites and rituals, one has to be cautious when using the epithets 'pragmatic' and 'utilitarian' to qualify Buddhism in its entirety. Because, the use of these two terms would tempt one to consider that Buddhism is on par with two contemporary philosophical systems known as pragmatism and utilitarianism. There may be, of course, some philosophical tenets common to all the three systems. Nevertheless, when taken as developed philosophical systems, fundamentally they are different from one another. Therefore the use of these two terms in relation to Buddhism is ambiguous. Apparently, in Buddhist context, they are to be understood in their general sense. Hence, in order to avoid any confusion, it is plausible to understand what these two systems of philosophy are.

Utilitarianism and Pragmatism: An Overview

The English philosophers Jeremy Bentham (1748-1832) and John Stuart Mill (1808-1873) were the initial exponents of utilitarianism, which attempts to lay down an objective principle for determining whether a given action is right or wrong. Principally, an action is right insofar as it tends to produce the greatest happiness for

---

[5]   *Buddhism its Essence and Development*, pp. 15-6

the greatest number. Although later we find deviations from the original interpretation, both of them interpreted 'happiness' as a form of hedonistic pleasure. Hence the theory amounts to saying that an action is right if it is productive of the greatest amount of pleasure for the greatest number; otherwise it is wrong. Essentially, utilitarianism is a philosophy, which lays stress upon the effects of an action. If an action bears beneficial results over harmful ones, then it is considered right. The most noteworthy thing in this connection is the separation of motive and intention from an action. As they argue, Hitler might have acted with good intention to improve Germany, but his action led to torture, genocide of Jews and created panic all over the world, ultimately ruining Germany itself. Therefore his action is not a utilitarian one. Thus utilitarianism as a moral theory distinguishes the rightness or the wrongness of an action from the goodness or badness of a doer who performs the action.

Charles Saunders Peirce (1839-1914) and William James (1842-1910) are the founders of pragmatism, which later elaborated by John Dewey (1859-1952) and others. Pragmatism is a philosophy developed against traditional philosophical thought. Just after the Civil War, young America was vigorously looking for a philosophy conducive to their march toward progress. They argued that traditional philosophy was separated from daily life and needs. The immediate concern of the new nation was to find a new philosophy, which would harness them to attain success. Therefore they formulated the new theory as a method of solving intellectual problems. Theories, according to them, are instruments; the problems must be solved with their help. Since a theory is true only if it can solve problems, a true theory has a pragmatic value. The criterion of judging the truth-value of a theory is science. There is a relationship between truth and good, and that which yields good results in terms of experience is a pragmatic truth. It was Dewy who developed the theory considerably in many respects.

Buddhism as a Way of Practice

Now, with this background in mind, we can probe into the Buddhist canonical texts to see how far it is pragmatic and utilitarian and not as elaborated in these two systems of philosophy, but in the general application of the terms in common use. Buddhism is pragmatic, because it envisages a practicable way for practice. It is utilitarian, because it enunciates only what is useful to practise for the realisation of the goal. Time and again the Buddha proclaimed the utilitarian and pragmatic values of the doctrine with emphatic terms.

In the very first discourse, where the Four Noble Truths are introduced for the first time, it is stated that those truths have three circles (*tiparivatta*) and twelve modes (*dvādasākāra*). The knowledge of each Noble Truth is one of the three circles amounting to four modes. Then with regard to the First Truth, it should be comprehended (*pariññeyyaṁ*) and has been comprehended (*pariññātaṁ*). The Second should be abandoned (*pahātabbaṁ*) and has been abandoned (*pahīnaṁ*). The Third should be realised (*sacchikātabbaṁ*) and has been realised (*sacchikataṁ*) and the Fourth should be developed (*bhāvetabbaṁ*) and has been developed (*bhāvitaṁ*). The analysis of these twelve modes would substantiate the fact that the teaching of the Buddha is not a mere philosophical hypothesis, but a doctrine to be understood and practised. Therefore the knowledge and practice of these twelve modes are known as 'seeing things as they really are' (*yathābhūtañāṇadassana*).

The ethical summary of the Teaching found in the *Dhammapada* illustrates its pragmatic nature more explicitly:

> "Abstention from all evil, cultivation of good and purification of one's mind – this is the Teaching of the Buddhas".

> (*Sabbapāpassa akaraṇaṁ –*
> *kusalassa upasampadā*
> *Sacittapariyodapanaṁ –*
> *etaṁ buddhanasāsanaṁ*)[6].

Then again it is stressed:

> "Striving should be done by yourselves, the Tathagatas are only teachers. The meditative ones, who enter the way, are delivered from the bonds of *Māra*".

> (*Tumhehi kiccaṁ ātappaṁ –*
> *akkhātāro Tathāgatā*
> *Paṭipannā pamokkhanti –*
> *jhāyino māra bandhanā*)[7].

Mere recitation of the scriptures without practice is criticised and the person who engages only in recitation is compared to a cowherd who does not derive the benefit of rearing cows:

---

[6] *Dhp.* 183
[7] *Dhp.* 276

"Though much he recites the Sacred Texts, but acts not accordingly, that heedless man is like a cowherd who counts others' kine. He has no share in the holy life".

(Bahum'pi ce sahitaṁ bhāsamāno –
na takkaro hoti naro pamatto
Gopo'va gāvo gaṇyaṁ paresaṁ –
na bhāgavā sāmaññassa hoti)[8]

In the same tone, it is said that the wise, by degrees, little by little, from time to time, should remove their taints, just as a smith removes the dross of silver.[9] In Buddhist ethical conduct, until one realises the supreme state, one is called a moral trainee (*sekha*), because he is still on the path of practice. Only after the realisation of the objective he is called a moral adept (*asekha*). The Buddha's call to practise the Dhamma is again found in the *Dhammadāyāda-sutta* of the *Majjhima-nikaya*:

"Meditate, O monks, under these foot of trees and in these remote lodgings lest you repent afterwards".

In the *Alagaddūpama-sutta*, it has been stated categorically with the Parable of the Raft that the doctrine should be taken as a means to an end and not to be taken as an end in itself. Herein, we are reminded of William James, who asserted that theories should be instruments to solve the problems of day to day life. Buddhism speaks of its threefold characteristic: Learning (*pariyatti*), Practice (*paṭipatti*) and Realisation (*paṭivedha*). These three are related to one another.

---

[8] *Dhp.* 19
[9] *Dhp.* 239

There would not be practice without learning and realisation without practice. The self-same pragmatic approach is seen in the description of Gradual Discipline (*anupubbasikkhā*), Gradual Action (*anupubbakiriyā*) and Gradual Training (*anupubbapaṭipadā*).

📖📖📖

Zen Master on Pragmatism

A Zen monk was sitting in Meditation once for a whole day. His Master asked him what he sought.

"My desire is to become a Buddha," said the monk.

Master picked up a piece of brick and began to polish it on a stone. Asked to explain his action, the Master said he wished to make a mirror.

"But no amount of polishing a brick will make it into a mirror," said the monk.

"If so, no amount of sitting cross-legged will make thee into a Buddha."

-Surekha V. Limaye
Zen (Buddhism) and Mysticism, p.56

No Anthropological Dimension in Buddhism

"So far as early Buddhism is concerned it does not present the essential aspects of antique religions, as illustrated in Egypt, Babylon and Mohenjodaro; it is developed form of religion. Hence the anthropological investigations into the origins of religions are more applicable to the Indus Valley religion and the earliest strata of the Vedic religion than to the Tipitaka Buddhism."

-Vishvanath Prasad Varma
Early Buddhism and its Origins, pp.27-8

20. An Evaluation of Buddhism as a Philosophy and a Religion

Buddhism, among other religions, cults and religious belief systems, is one of the world religions possessing a history of well over two and a half millennia. It started in a specific period in a particular territory in the Indian subcontinent by a unique human personality popularly known as Buddha. He was born to human parents and lived an exemplary earthly life, inspiring an awareness in others 'to be oneself' and 'strive for one's own betterment' by oneself'. In consideration of His extraordinary conduct and wisdom with which He addressed to human reason, He was and still is honoured as an incomparable Teacher of humankind the world has ever produced. Since the doctrine that He preached for forty-five years of His earthly career is based on a theory discovered by Himself and is related to practice, it is both philosophical and religious in popular applications of the terms and is known collectively as Buddhism.

What is Philosophy?

As we know today, philosophy is one of the academic disciplines for higher studies in the world over. Since the subject of philosophy, in the course of centuries, has grown out of proportion, it has been departmentalised into five branches of study. They are known as metaphysics, ethics, aesthetics, epistemology and logic. Metaphysics, having two subdivisions called ontology and cosmology, deals with first principles, and therefore, deviates from Buddhism's approach to reality. Buddhism abounds in ethical and aesthetic exhortations particular to itself together with a cogent presentation of epistemological data on a sound footing. Regarding logic, Buddhism adheres to induction while finding fault with deduction as a valid means of knowledge. However, on an empirical level, logical coherence and consistency of propositions are encouraged for better understanding, but speculative reasoning and abstractions on such reasoning are discouraged. Besides, in some instances, dialectics, too, has been employed as a logical apparatus for the purpose of highlighting the pragmatic aspect of His doctrine. Buddhism has interest in neither ontology nor cosmology; however, the descriptions of planes of existence found in the canonical texts, are referred to as Buddhist cosmology by some writers. In philosophical studies cosmology is a study of the origin and structure of the universe. Since the Buddhist description of planes of existence does not deal with the origin or structure of the universe, Buddhism has no cosmology in the sense that it has been used in philosophy.

The English word 'philosophy' is derived from a Greek term meaning 'love of knowledge or wisdom'. Nevertheless, at present, apart from using it to introduce the discipline known by the name 'philosophy', the term is used to denote, 'an attitude toward certain activity and concepts underlying academic disciplines'. Therefore the term is popularly used together with other disciplines such as history, law, religion, sociology and so on to name the underlying train of thought of those subjects, e. g., philosophy of history, philosophy of law, philosophy of religion and philosophy of sociology. When we take philosophy as a separate branch of study with its subdivisions, it being a sort of mental adventure is built on speculative reasoning that probes into things beyond our phenomenal experience. Particularly, metaphysics in philosophy is curiosity motivated. Therefore, C. E. M. Joad, answering the question posed by himself, "Why we study philosophy?" asserts:

> "There is only one answer to the question. To satisfy the impulse of curiosity"[1]

Is Buddhism a Philosophy?

The Pali word '*diṭṭhi*' stands for philosophy, and literally means 'a view'. Two kinds of views are distinguished: Wrong View (*micchā diṭṭhi*) and Right View (*sammā diṭṭhi*). While Wrong View hinders one's path to liberation, Right View lights up one's path. Very often than not a speculative view is characterised as 'thicket of views, the wilderness of views, the contortion of views, the vacillation of views and the fetter of views'. And further it is stated that because of a view adhered to by an untaught ordinary person, he is not freed from birth, ageing, death, sorrow, lamentation, pain, grief and despair. In short, he is not freed from the mass of suffering he is presently undergoing. (See *M.* I, p. 9). Right View is, however, equated with 'vision' (*dassana*). Therefore a Buddhist is advised to give up views and to be endowed with vision (*diṭṭhiṁ ca anupagamma dassanena sampanno*). It is well known how the Buddha analysed sixty-two philosophical views in the *Brahmajāla-sutta* of the *Digha-nikāya*. All those views were in vogue in contemporary India, the Buddha rejected them on the ground that they were mere views or speculative philosophies serving no substantial purpose.

---

[1]   Joad C.E., *Philosophy*, p. 16

If we mean 'love of knowledge or wisdom' by the word 'philosophy' in conformity with its etymological meaning, certainly Buddhism can be termed as a philosophy. It unfolds a theory leading to wisdom. The path of practice envisaged in Buddhism culminates in wisdom, which is otherwise called 'insight'. Among different kinds of philosophical systems in the world, Buddhism occupies a unique position. It is not a philosophy as philosophy per se. Since it is a practical philosophy, it has not engaged in mere speculation on man and his destiny. It points out a way for his perfection, which is to be practised in his daily life. It is a philosophy with a tinge of morality influencing man's conduct.

What is Religion?

The word 'religion' is defined in dictionaries with a theistic bias. According to dictionaries, therefore, it is a system of beliefs, reposing confidence in a supernatural being. The definitions given in dictionaries, however, do not exhaust all forms of worship and moral practices known by the term 'religion' today. When we examine world religions individually, we see that Buddhism is devoid of two fundamentals found in almost all the religions known to us. They are the concept of a creator god and the theory of Soul. It is believed that the concept of god in monotheistic sense has originated from polytheism as in India, Greece and Rome. Later, god was conceived not only as the architect of the universe, but also as one who actively intervened in natural forces and the destiny of humanity. Brahmanism (later Hinduism), Judaism, Christianity and Islam claim that god is revealed in their scriptures. Christian theology adduces several arguments to prove the existence god, which have been thoroughly examined and criticised by independent thinkers. Buddhism dismisses the theory of creation as a myth and refutes the concept of First Cause or Uncaused Cause, the name given to god, on the basis of Buddhist teaching called Causal Genesis. Soul theory has taken different forms in different religions. Some religions speak of a macrocosmic soul and a microcosmic soul, the latter is said to be merged with the macrocosmic soul at the end. Yet some other religions say that it is the manikin in man, which is saved by god for eternal life. Buddhism rejects all forms of views on soul and classifies the human person into five aggregates and establishes the facts of impermanence and suffering related to aggregates.

Religion began with primitive life, probably with animistic beliefs and magic, and evolved throughout human civilisation. Sociologist Reece McGee identified four types of religions existing today:

1. Simple supernaturalism
2. Animism
3. Theism
4. Transcendental idealism

Since Buddhism emphasises good conduct and self-culture directed towards a transcendental ideal state, it falls into the fourth type. As it is ethical from beginning to the end, it envisages ethical and moral practice in every phase of man's pilgrimage to perfection. It is a religion free from either monotheism or monism. It provides a graduated course of moral action for the realisation of the ideal it objectifies. Radhakrisnan in his 'Indian Philosophy' named Buddhism as 'Ethical Idealism'.

Buddhism as a Religion

Whatever be the dictionary meaning given to the term 'religion' from the Western angle, Buddhism is recognised as a world religion. Apart from the belief of an almighty god to whom one should pray for one's salvation and the concept of soul, Buddhism entertains many of the characteristics of a religion. It lays down a mode of practice (*paṭipadā*) for the adherent to follow, which is popularly known as 'Middle Path' (*majjhimā paṭipadā*). He or she is obliged to observe Buddhist practice, which governs his or her conduct. Religiosity and the practice begin with the avowed pronouncement of allegiance to go to the refuge of the Buddha, the doctrine and the community of monks. Then he or she becomes a male or female lay devotee (*upāsaka* or *upāsikā*) following the religion preached by the Buddha. The word literally means 'one who sits nearby' (from *upa+√as* to sit). By observing the five elementary precepts, he becomes a virtuous adherent. This fact was made clear by the Buddha to Mahanama, the Sakyan who inquired the Buddha:

"Lord, how a person becomes a lay disciple?"

"When, Mahanama, a person has found refuge in the Buddha, found refuge in the Dhamma, found refuge in the Order, then that person is a lay disciple."

"Lord, how is a lay disciple virtuous?"

"When, Mahanama, a lay disciple abstains from taking life; abstains from taking what is not given; abstains from sexual misconduct; abstains from lying; and abstains from intoxicating drinks, which causes indolence; then a lay disciple is virtuous."[2]

By taking refuge in the Buddha, Dhamma and Sangha, one tends to become morally obliged to undertake the responsibility of observing the precepts resulting in him to be born in a heavenly world.[3] Because of evil conduct in body, word and mind, one is bound to be born in a woeful state.[4] This shows that Buddhism is a religion enunciating a way of life.

📖📖📖

Why is Religion Blended with Philosophy?

"In other words, the aim of studying philosophy is not merely to gratify theoretical curiosity, however disinterested that curiosity may be; it is also to live the right kind of life, consciously adjusting one's conduct to one's intellectual convictions. It is in this sense of dogma or superstition, that religion is blended with philosophy in India."

-M. Hiriyanna
The Essentials of Indian Philosophy, pp.25-6

---

[2]   *A.* III. p. 220
[3]   *S.* IV, p. 270
[4]   *A.* I. p. 56

"Patirūpakārī Ḍhuravā
Uṭṭhātā Vindate Ḍhanaṁ"

"Toiling - rejoicing - sorrowing,
Onward through life he goes;
Each morning sees some task begin,
Each evening sees its close;
Something attempted, something done,
Has earned a night's repose.

Thanks, thanks to thee, my worthy friend,
For the lesson thou hast taught!
Thus at the flaming forge of our life
Our fortunes must be wrought;
Thus on its sounding anvil shaped
Each burning deed and thought!"

-Henry Wadsworth Longfellow
The Village Blacksmith

21. Uses and Abuses of Wealth

People very often speak of economic crisis that dominates every quarter of the world. What they mean to say is business enterprises and economic management are experiencing tremendous setbacks creating financial difficulties for everyone in both commercial and private sectors in society.

Market economy, the legacy of industrialization, has jeopardized economic activity in many parts of the world in many respects due to reasons beyond the control of industrial magnates and the respective states. The problem is how to find an antidote to alleviate this woe of business entrepreneurs and the common people.

Behind depression, there can be some "invisible manipulative powers" as well as some exorbitant measures taken by a government. But on the personal level, let us look at the problem in Buddhist perspective and see how far man himself is responsible for the situation in which he thinks that he is denied of 'affluent lifestyle' and what could be man's contribution to remedy the situation. We can see that this is an age-old woe based on man's insatiable desire originated from his hoarding consciousness.

What is to be noted in this regard is the Buddhist paradigm in economic management, which is totally applicable to everyone and every business undertaking beginning from small-scale personal ventures to large-scale multi-million dollar enterprises.

Facing the Situation with Understanding

When we look at the problem from the angle which the Buddha has viewed and analyzed, gain and loss are two out of eight vicissitudes of life, otherwise known as worldly conditions *(lokadhamma)* that every one of us has to experience invariably as social beings. It is stated in the often quoted *Mangala-sutta* that when affected by these vicissitudes, if one's mind is not perturbed, it is the state of security free from sorrow and free from taints.[1]

Gain and loss, just as much as fame and disrepute, praise and blame, happiness and sorrow, are component parts of human experience. Hence they come under the generic Buddhist term *'dukkha'*. One is advised to condition one's mind to face the situation with understanding. Human problems are everywhere. Just as they are here in the present, they were there in the past and will be there in time to come, too. What the Buddha has said some two and half millenniums ago on economic management to those who sought his advice, when taken out from contemporary Indian context, is therefore, relevant even to modern society. Since human greed extends beyond the bounds of human needs in alarming proportions, man is ever bound to experience dissatisfaction and disappointment in the ventures he has undertaken.

Among the fifteen character-building qualities in the *Metta-sutta,* the Buddha delineated four qualities to be cultivated by one who is treading the Buddhist path. They are directly connected with ameliorating the financial woes of any individual. Accordingly, one should be contented *(santussaka)*, easily supportable *(subhara)*,

---

[1] *Sn.* p.46 ff.

of less undertaking *(appakicca)* and of simple living *(sallahukavutti).* [2]

In Buddhist sense, contentment does not mean lack of interest or impassivity or inaction in any venture amounting to doing nothing for one's own progress. It is the quality of the mind that prepares one to face both advantageous and disadvantageous situations with equal satisfaction. In order to keep one's head above water one ought to know the limits of one's needs. We may be having many wants, but less needs. Therefore what is necessary is to readjust one's mindset more for one's needs above wants and tailor the wants to possible minimum limit. Insatiable desire for wants may lead one to utter disappointment. When one understands the reality that life in the world is incomplete, insatiable, the slave of craving,[3] one is more eligible to face the situation with understanding.

The Blueprint of Successful Living

Let us see what the Buddha has said to Dighajanu the Kolian, when he called on the Buddha. Dighajanu said:

> "We householders are immersed in the round of pleasure. We are encumbered with our consorts and children. We delight in muslin and sandalwood from Benares. We deck ourselves with flowers. Lord, such as us, let the Exalted One teach Dhamma which will be to our advantage and happiness here on earth and for

---

[2] Sn. 144
[3] " ūno loko atitto taṇhādāso" - M. II, p.67

our advantage and happiness in the next world after death."

So the Buddha in response to his request, preached four conditions advantageous for this life and four for the next life. Since they mainly involve economic activity, herein let us examine the four conditions that contribute to happiness in this life. Even at a glance, one can see not only the relevance of these conditions in the form of guidelines to man's economic life, but also the clarity and precision with which they have been preached.

1. Achievement in alertness
   (*uṭṭhānasampadā*)
2. Achievement in conservation
   (*ārakkhahasampadā*)
3. Good company (*kalyānamittatā*)
4. Even life (*samajīvikatā*)

According to the first condition, a person who earns his living whether by tilling the soil or by cattle-rearing or by archery or by service to the state or by any of the crafts, he must be energetic, tireless and gifted with an inquiring turn of mind into ways and means of doing the work in hand. He must be capable of carrying out his job with interest and perseverance. He mobilizes his energy for the achievement of best of results. It is "he who is energetic, bears the burden and does what is befitting enjoys wealth".[4]

The second condition deals with the conservation of what is earned by effort and zeal, collected by the strength of one's arm and by the sweat of one's brow, justly obtained in a lawful manner. The third speaks of

---

[4] "patirūpakāri dhuravā - uṭṭhātā vindate dhanaṁ - Sn. 187

the association with friends who are morally good and sound of heart. The fourth, 'even life', deals with an admonition to balance one's budget. The clansman who experiences gain and loss should continue his business serenely, not being unduly elated in high income or depressed by low income. He should be vigilant in observing that his expenditure does not exceed his income. Without being miserly or extravagant, he must be attentive to make both ends meet. Both inlets and outlets of one's income and expenditure have to be watched with attention to minimize waste.

A Man for All Seasons

Out of these four conditions, 1, 2 and 4 deal with personal factors of alertness, conservation and spending which are to be devised by personal motivation. The third is the social factor that boosts one's self-confidence to be considerate in associating friends, a fact that has been analyzed in the Buddhist teaching in numerous instances. Together the four guidelines characterize a man for all seasons.

The Buddha, describing the fourth condition, draws a clear-cut line between the two extremes of extravagant expenditure and miserliness. It is stated that a person having small earnings and lives on a grand scale uses up his wealth as a 'fig-tree glutton' *(udumbarakhādaka)*, who being desirous of eating fig fruits, shakes the tree violently, causing many fruits to fall, ripe and raw. Not to speak of the raw fruits, a large part of the ripe fruits is also wasted. Because of one's extravagant lifestyle, one soon exhausts what is in one's coffers just as the 'fig-tree glutton'. A person having a great income and lives stingily without spending even for bare necessities, will die like a starveling *(ajaddhumārika)*, hapless and neglected. Therefore one who abstains from both squandering and stinginess and prone to make both ends meet is a man for all seasons.

Economic Planning

According to Buddhism, there is nothing wrong in becoming rich, but in Buddhism, the means by which one becomes rich and the way by which one should use one's riches are taken into consideration. In the Dhammapada it is stated that one who has not lived the moral life and not earned wealth in youth keeps on brooding in one's old age like an old heron at a muddy pond, and also like a worn out bow sighing after past.[5] In the *Sigālovāda-sutta*, the layman is specifically asked to earn wealth even as bees collecting honey and termites building an anthill and spend it wisely. It runs thus:

> "To him amassing wealth, like roving bee
> Its honey gathering and hurting naught
> Riches mount up as ant-heap growing high.
> When the good layman wealth has so amassed
> Able is he to benefit his clan
> In portion four let him divide that wealth
> So binds him to himself life's friendly things.
>
> One portion let him spend and taste the fruit.
> His business to conduct let him take two
> And portion four let him reserve and hoard;
> So there will be wherewithal in times of needs".

[5] Dhp. 155, 156

One might think that the economic planning together with saving for future use as envisaged by the Buddha are directly contrasted with the Buddhist concept of renunciation. It is certainly not so. Renunciation is one thing, leading a happy family life is another. Buddhism is sometimes misrepresented as a religion of pessimistic outlook having a world-negating attitude. Buddhism is not a religion solely for a monastic community, it embraces lay (both male and female) community as well. Therefore this is one of the glaring instances where the Buddha has shown how economic planning is inevitable for economic security of any individual in society.

The investment of two portions of one's earnings is recommended in anticipation of a better income to meet the demands in time to come. A portion of the income is to be deposited for use during unexpected calamities, which would help one to be at ease in future being free from thoughts of foreboding. It may be like purchasing insurance policies or depositing in banks. As the commentary explains, one fourth of one's income is to be taken not only for one's own subsistence but also for other petty expenses and to help the needy and to give away in charity.[6] In fact, a person who while being economically sound does not maintain his aged parents is termed as a man of mean character.[7]

Since economic planning is so indispensable to leading a happy and successful lay life, the Buddha pointed out to the millionaire Anathapindika, economic stability *(atthisukha)* which results from proper management and just and righteous enterprises *(anavajjasukha)* are contributory to one's happiness. Enjoying the bliss of not

---

[6] DA. III, Sec. 265 - Chaṭṭhasangāyanā, CD-ROM
[7] Sn. 125

being indebted *(ananasukha)* one must be able to enjoy one's wealth with friends and relatives *(bhogasukha)*. Sharing of one's wealth with the needy and the clergy are highly commended virtues in Buddhist ethics.[8]

The Uses and Abuses of Wealth

As it is depicted in the canonical scriptures, the Buddha is also concerned not only with the uses, but the abuses of one's earnings as well. Explaining the Achievement of Generosity *(cāgasampadā)* to the millionaire, the Buddha outlines the ways of utilizing one's wealth profitably, not only for one's own benefit, but for others' benefit as well.[9] As described further in the Buddha's address, 'one has to live at home with heart free from taint of stinginess, open-handed, pure-handed, delighting in self-surrender, being a person to ask a favour of, and dispensing charitable gifts'. Certainly, wealth is to be rightfully and lawfully earned. 'It is to be acquired by energetic striving, amassed by strength of arm, won by sweat, lawful and lawfully gotten' and not by exploitation of labour or by illegal trafficking of any kind or by any fraudulent means like black marketing or smuggling or embezzlement. With the wealth thus justly acquired 'he makes himself secure against all misfortunes whatsoever, such as may happen by way of fire, water, the king, a robber, an ill disposed person or (expectant) heir, and devises defense and security for him'.

Now, what is more convincing in this respect is, the Buddha's explanation of how to put one's earnings into

---

[8] A. II, p.68
[9] A. II, p. 66

use. In this connection, the Buddha explains the issue on four heads:

1. With the wealth one has lawfully earned, he makes the mother, father, wife and children, servants and workmen, friends and comrades happy.

2. He makes himself secure against all misfortunes such as may happen by way of fire, water, the king, robber and ill disposed person.

3. He performs fivefold offerings (*bali*): to relatives (*ñāti*), to guests (*athiti*), to departed ones (*pubbapeta*),to kings (*rāja*) and to deities (*devatā*).

4. He gives away in charity to recluses and brahmins who practise abstinence from sloth and negligence, who are bent on kindness and forbearance, who strive to tame, calm and cool themselves from defilement.[10]

The wealth of anyone spent without these four deeds of merits is called wealth that has failed to seize its opportunity, failed to win merits and unfittingly used. In many a dialogue of the Buddha, ways of abusing money are detailed. In sociological perspective, dissipating earnings amounts to a crime without victims. Nevertheless, abuse of wealth ruins oneself at the beginning and then leaves its impact on society at the end. People abuse their wealth not only by hoarding, but

---

[10] A. II, p.67

also using it extravagantly in pursuit of cheap sensual satisfaction, which are discussed in the *Sigālovada-sutta* under Six Doors to Woe (*cha apāyamukha*). On the personal level as well as social level, adultery, addiction to drugs and alchoholc drinks, gambling, bad company and numerous other vices detrimental to one's own and society's welfare are considered abuses of wealth. A person proud and snobbish (*dhanatthaddha*) due to his riches also abuses his wealth by neglecting what is to be done thereby causing his own downfall.[11] The vanity of such thoughts is shown with emphatic phraseology. For it is stated: " A fool may worry thinking that he has sons and wealth but actually speaking, when he himself is not his own, how can there be sons and wealth?"[12]

Black Money, Dirty Money and Easy Money

There is an important discourse addressed to a headman called Rasiya where the accumulation of wealth is discussed with reference to the Middle Path. Rasiya, in front of the Buddha, poses the question whether the Buddha censures and abuses downright all kinds of asceticism and ascetics who lead austere ascetic mode of life. Herein the Buddha asserts, those who represent him as one who censures and abuses downright all kinds of ascetic practices who lead austere ascetic mode of life are wrong and do not speak in accordance with his view but misrepresent him. Then explaining the extreme practice of self-indulgence as low, vulgar, practice of the many-folk, ignoble and not bound up with welfare, explains the self-mortification, as painful, ignoble and not bound up with welfare. The explanation is just the same as the

[11] Sn. 104
[12] Dhp. 62

one we find in the first discourse, the Turning of the
Wheel of Law. Then proceeds on to outline the Noble
Eightfold Path and describes the means by which people
earn and make use of wealth.

The discourse is important for two reasons. Firstly, it
points out the commendable mode of conduct in relation
to the Middle Path avoiding two extremes. Secondly, it
delineates the relevance of the Middle Path to every
aspect of a layman's life. Now, in accordance with the
means that common-folk employ to earn wealth, they fall
into three categories:

1.   Those who employ unlawful and violent
     means.

2.   Those who employ both unlawful and
     lawful means.

3.   Those who employ only lawful means.

In regard to the first and second categories of people,
wealth earned by unlawful and violent means is
illegitimate and illegal, and considered as black, dirty and
easy money, which is blameworthy; whereas the second
and third categories, what is lawfully earned is legal,
legitimate, righteous and praiseworthy. In the long
analysis of the issue found in the discourse, Buddha
criticises the illegal means of acquisition in spite of the
fact that it is spent generously for others' welfare.

Thus money, for that matter, wealth or property is not an
end in itself. Until one thinks that it is only a means to an
end, one is ever in disappointment. Hoarding
consciousness or extravagant lifestyle leads one nowhere.
The most deplorable thing in our society is, man is

subjected to the demands of modern living over and above social norms and values. As long as he is alienated from his moral character, he is bound to experience difficulties in economic management for a contented living.

📖📖📖

Everybody's Religion

"When it is a question of money, everybody is of the same religion."

-Voltaire

For Further Reading:

Chapter 1

- Piyadassi Ven. – *The Buddha's Ancient Path*, Chap. 1- *The Buddha*, pp. 11-22.
- Narada Ven. – *The Buddha and His Teachings*, Chap. 1 – *The Buddha,* pp. 1-233 (A comprehensive account on Birth, renunciation, struggle for Enlightenment, lineage, relatives, ministry and daily routine is given in this chapter).
- Gnanarama P. Ven. – *The Mission Accomplished*, Chap. 8 – *Traces of Docetic Elements*, pp. 80-96 (The chapter deals with some of the misconceptions of Western Buddhist scholars who conjectured that the Buddha never existed, and the supernatural elements that grew around the historical Buddha).
- Thomas E.J. – *The Life of Buddha*, pp. 1-61. (Here the author deals with the life of Buddha on materials drawn from Pali canonical scriptures).

Chapter 2

- Wijesekara O.H.DeA. - *The Three Signata, Anicca, Dukkha, Anatta*, Buddhist Publication Society, Kandy. (This booklet gives a brief but an authoritative account of the three characteristics)
- *The Basic Facts of Existence I,* collected Essays, Buddhist Publication Society, Kandy. (Essay written by Ven. Bhikkhu Ñāṇajiviko is an approach to the topic of impermanence from the standpoint of modern Western philosophy)
- Narada Ven. - The *Buddha and His Teachings*, pp.543-551

Chapter 3

- Wijesekara O.H.DeA. – *The Three Signata, Anicca, Dukkha, Anatta;* Buddhist Publication Society, Kandy.
- Narada Ven. – *The Buddha and His Teachings,* Chap. 16, pp.313-322
- Piyadassi Ven. – *The Buddha's Ancient Path,* Chap. 3, pp.37-53 (This chapter provides a very comprehensive account on the topic)

Chapter 4

- Rahula W. Ven.– *What the Buddha Taught,* Chap. VI, The Doctrine of No-Soul, pp. 51-66
- *The Three Basic Facts of Existence III* (A collection of articles on the Buddhist teaching of egolessness and its interpretation by eminent Buddhist scholars, Buddhist Publication Society, Kandy, Sri Lanka.)
- Nyanatiloka Ven. – *Buddhist Dictionary* (on *'anatta'*)
- Malalasekera G.P. - *The Truth of Anatta* (Wheel 94, published by Buddhist Publication Society, Kandy, Sri Lanka.)
- Hiriyanna M. – *Outlines of Indian Philosophy,* Chap. 2, pp. 48-83

Chapter 5

- Rahula W. Ven. - *What the Buddha Taught,* Chap. I, pp. 16-29
- Piyadassi Ven. – *The Buddha's Ancient Path,* Chap. 3, pp. 37-53
- Thomas E.J. – *The Life of Buddha,* Chap. VII, pp.80-96
- Thouless Robert H. – *Christianity and Buddhism,* p. 5 (Buddhist Research Society, Singapore)

Chapter 6
- Rahula W. Ven. – *What the Buddha Taught*, pp. 29-34
- Piyadassi Ven. - *The Buddha's Ancient Path,* pp. 37-53
- Narada Ven. – *The Buddha and His Teachings,* pp. 84, 90, 325-6

Chapter 7
- Narada Ven. – *The Buddha and His Teachings,* Chaps. 34, 35, pp. 490-511
- Piyadassi Ven. – *The Buddha's Ancient Path,* Chap. 5, pp. 67-76
- Rahula W. Ven. – *What the Buddha Taught,* Cap. IV, pp. 35-44

Chapter 8
- Piyadassi Ven. – *The Buddha's Ancient Path*, Chap. 7-14, pp.87-218 (A detailed account on the Noble Eightfold Path is given in this book)
- Narada Ven. – *The Buddha and His Teachings,* Chap. 17, pp. 323-332
- Rahula W. Ven. – *What the Buddha Taught,* Chap. V, pp. 45-50

Chapter 9
- Narada Ven. – *The Buddha and His Teachings,* Chap. 25. pp. 419- 432. The chapter gives a detailed description of the Interdependent Origination.
- Jayatilleke K.N. – *Early Buddhist Theory of Knowledge,* Sections 762- 788, pp. 445-461. The sections discuss the theories of causation in different Indian philosophical systems and provide an exhaustive study on the subject. He shows how the

theory has been misunderstood by the Western scholars.

Chapter 10

- Narada Ven. – *The Buddha and His Teachings,* Chap.27, pp. 436-445
- Baptist Egerton C. - *31 Planes of Existence* , Buddhist Cultural Centre, Colombo (The book deals with the abodes of beings in detail)
- Narada Ven. – *Manual of Abhidhamma,* pp. 234-246, Singapore Buddhist Meditation Centre
  (Span of life in each plane is described here)
- Jayatilleke K.N. – *Facets of Buddhist Thought.* BPS, Kandy, Sri Lanka (The first essay of this booklet entitled *'The Buddhist Conception of the Universe'* is a scientific study of the material on world systems found in Pali canonical texts of the Theravada tradition)
- Gnanarama P. Ven. – *The Mission Accomplished,* pp. 145-146
  (A short note on devas)

Chapter 11

- Jayatillake K.N. – *Ethics in Buddhist Perspective* pp. 1-14, BPS, Sri Lanka
- Dharmasiri Gunapala Prof. – *A Buddhist Critique of the Christian Concept of God.* p. 42 and 45ff.
- Gnanarama P. Ven. – *An Approach to Buddhist Social Philosophy.* Chap. 2

Chapter 12

◆ Karunaratne W.S. – *Buddhism its Religion and Philosophy, Chap. 14*, pp.94-113, The Buddhist Research Society 1988, Singapore
◆ Jayatilleke K.N. – *Facets of Buddhist Thought*, pp. 76-91, The Wheel Publication No. 162/ 163/ 164, BPS, Kandy, Sri Lanka

Chapter 13

◆ Jayatilleke K.N. – *Early Buddhist Theory of Knowledge,* Chapter VII on Logic and Truth and Chapter VIII on Authority and Reason Within Buddhism

Chapter 14

◆ Jayatilleke K.N. – *Ethics in Buddhist Perspective*, Chap. IV, BPS, Sri Lanka
◆ Dharmasiri Gunapala – *Fundamentals of Buddhist Ethics*, Chap. 3, The Buddhist Research Society, Singapore
◆ Gnanarama P. Ven. – *Aspects of Early Buddhist Sociological Thought*, Chap. 7, Singapore

Chapter 15

◆ Jayatilleke K.N. – *Early Buddhist Theory of Knowledge*, p. 364 ff.

Chapter 16

◆ Jayatilleke K.N. – *Early Buddhist Theory of Knowledge*, pp. 453-461
◆ Radhakrishnan S. – *Indian Philosophy,* pp. 359-60
◆ Warder A.K. – *Indian Buddhism*, pp. 299-302

Chapter 17
- Jayatilleke K.N. – *Early Buddhist Theory of Knowledge*, pp. 402-3
- Radhakrishnan S. - *Indian Philosophy*, pp. 359-360
- Gnanarama P. Ven.– *Aspects of Early Buddhist Sociological Thought*, pp. 27-40

Chapter 18
- Wijesekera O.H.DeA. – *Buddhist and Vedic Studies*, Chap. 5, Buddhism and Society, pp. 53-70
- No. 41 *Sāleyyaka-sutta, Majjhima-nikaya*, Vol. I, pp. 285 ff.

Chapter 19
- Jayatilleke K.N. – *Early Buddhist Theory of Knowledge*, p. 357 ff., p. 471
- Hiriyanna M. – *Outlines of Indian Philosophy*, pp. 137-147

Chapter 20
- Gnanarama P. Ven. – *Aspects of Early Buddhist Sociological Thought*, Chap. 1, pp. 1-45
- Conze Edward – *Buddhism: Its Essence and Development*, Introduction, pp. 11-18

Chapter 21
- Schumarcher E.F. - *Small is Beautiful,* under "*Buddhist Economics*", pp. 38-46
- Gnanarama P. Ven. - *An Approach to Buddhist Social Philosophy*, Chap. 10 - *The Buddhist Attitude to Poverty, Wealth and Economic Resources,* pp. 126-140

A.	Anguttara Nikāya
AA.	Anguttara Nikāya Aṭṭhakathā *(Manorathapūraṇi)*
D.	Digha Nikāya
DA.	Digha Nikāya Aṭṭhakathā *(Sumangalavilāsini)*
DB	Dialogues of the Buddha
Dhp.	Dhammapada
DhpA.	Dhammapada Aṭṭhakathā
DhSA	Dhammasangani Aṭṭhakathā
DPPN.	Dictionary of Pali Proper Names
EBTK	Early Buddhist Theory of Knowledge
IB	Indian Buddhism
IPh	Indian Philosophy
It.	Itivuttaka
KhpA.	Khuddakapāṭha Aṭṭhakathā
KS	Kindred Sayings
M.	Majjhima Nikāya
MA.	Majjhima Nikāya Aṭṭhakathā *(Papañcasūdani)*
Mil.	Milindapañha
MLDB	Middle Length Dialogues of the Buddha
MLS	Middle Length Sayings
OIPh	Outlines of Indian Philosophy
PTS	Pali Text Society
S.	Samyutta Nikāya
SA.	Samyutta Nikāya Aṭṭhakathā *(Sāratthappakāsini)*
Sn.	Suttanipāta
SnA.	Suttanipāta Aṭṭhakathā *(Paramattha-jotikā)*
The Path	The Path of Purification
Ud.	Udāna
UdA.	Udāna Aṭṭhakathā *(Paramatthadīpani)*
Vin.	Vinaya
VinA.	Vinaya Aṭṭhakathā *(Samantapāsādikā)*
Vis.	Visuddhimagga

By the same author:

1. *Three Centuries after the Great Decease* (Sinhala)

2. *Plato* (Sinhala) co-author

3. *A Study of Jataka Tales* (Sinhala)

4. *An Approach to Buddhist Social Philosophy* (English)

5. *Early Buddhism and Problems of Interpretation* (Sinhala)

6. *The Mission Accomplished* (English)

7. *Aspects of Early Buddhist Sociological Thought* (English)

There has been a noticeable lack of a good textbook on Buddhism for university and college students. Ven.Gnanarama's book on *Essentials of Buddhism* meets this demand very successfully.

Ven. Gnanarama, with his long experience in teaching at universities and colleges both in Sri Lanka and abroad, is eminently suitable for this responsible task.

Prof. Gunapala Dharmasiri
Department of Philosophy
University of Peradeniya
Sri Lanka

A consistent and comprehensive treatise on *Essentials of Buddhism*.

Prof. Kapila Abhayawansa
Post Graduate Institute of
Pali and Buddhist Studies
University of Kelaniya
Sri Lanka

TAKING REFUGE IN THE TRIPLE JEWELS

To the Buddha I return and rely,
returning from delusions and
relying upon Awareness and Understanding.

To the Dharma I return and rely,
returning from erroneous views and
relying upon Proper Views and Understanding.

To the Sangha I return and rely,
returning from pollutions and disharmony and
relying upon Purity of Mind and
the Six Principles of Living in Harmony.

Be mindful of Amitabha!
Namo Amitabha!
Homage to Amita Buddha!

May every living being, drowning and adrift,
Soon return to the Pure Land of Limitless Light!

"Wherever the Buddha's teachings have flourished,
either in cities or countrysides,
people would gain inconceivable benefits.
The land and pepole would be enveloped in peace.
The sun and moon will shine clear and bright.
Wind and rain would appear accordingly,
and there will be no disasters.
Nations would be prosperous
and there would be no use for soldiers or weapons.
People would abide by morality and accord with laws.
They would be courteous and humble,
and everyone would be content without injustices.
There would be no thefts or violence.
The strong would not dominate the weak
and everyone would get their fair share."

~ THE BUDDHA SPEAKS OF
THE INFINITE LIFE SUTRA OF
ADORNMENT, PURITY, EQUALITY
AND ENLIGHTENMENT OF
THE MAHAYANA SCHOOL ~

With bad advisors forever left behind,
From paths of evil he departs for eternity,
Soon to see the Buddha of Limitless Light
And perfect Samantabhadra's Supreme Vows.

The supreme and endless blessings
of Samantabhadra's deeds,
I now universally transfer.
May every living being, drowning and adrift,
Soon return to the Pure Land of
Limitless Light!

~The Vows of Samantabhadra~

I vow that when my life approaches its end,
All obstructions will be swept away;
I will see Amitabha Buddha,
And be born in His Western Pure Land of
Ultimate Bliss and Peace.

When reborn in the Western Pure Land,
I will perfect and completely fulfill
Without exception these Great Vows,
To delight and benefit all beings.

~The Vows of Samantabhadra
Avatamsaka Sutra~

DEDICATION OF MERIT

May the merit and virtue
accrued from this work
adorn Amitabha Buddha's Pure Land,
repay the four great kindnesses above,
and relieve the suffering of
those on the three paths below.

May those who see or hear of these efforts
generate Bodhi-mind,
spend their lives devoted to the Buddha Dharma,
and finally be reborn together in
the Land of Ultimate Bliss.
Homage to Amita Buddha!

NAMO AMITABHA
南無阿彌陀佛

財團法人佛陀教育基金會 印贈
台北市杭州南路一段五十五號十一樓
Printed and donated for free distribution by
The Corporate Body of the Buddha Educational Foundation
11F., 55 Hang Chow South Road Sec 1, Taipei, Taiwan, R.O.C.
Tel: 886-2-23951198 , Fax: 886-2-23913415
Email: overseas@budaedu.org
Website:http://www.budaedu.org
This book is strictly for free distribution, it is not for sale.
Printed in Taiwan
20,000 copies; Jan 2004
EN159-3593